NOT

Our Father's Faith:
How Doctrines OF Demons
Have Invaded The Church

by
Bill Rudge

OFFICIAL DISCLOSURE

A DIVISION OF DEFENDER PUBLISHING

CRANE

Official Disclosure
A division of Defender Publishing House,
Crane 65633
Copyright 2010 by Bill Rudge
All rights reserved. Published 2010

Printed in the United States of America
10   1
ISBN-10: 0984061126 (paperback)
ISBN-13: 9780984061129 (paperback)

Cover design by Daniel M. Wright

A CIP catalog record for this book is available from
the Library of Congress.

Scripture quotations are from the King James Version of the Bible.
(Emphasis added to Scriptures are by the author.)

This book is the result of twenty years of research, countless hours of Scripture study, and thousands of hours in prayer and fasting. I could not have completed this arduous and crucial endeavor without the prayers and support of my wife, children, family, staff, and ministry friends. I especially thank the Lord for His inspiration, provision, protection, peace, power, and faithfulness.

CONTENTS

*My prayer is that you read this book with
an open Bible and a heart that is truly sensitive
and surrendered to the Spirit of God.*
Bill Rudge

Chapter One

SPIRITUAL IMMUNE DEFICIENCY RUNNING RAMPANT IN THE CHURCH TODAY

There is a strong delusion and dangerous deception infiltrating the Church today. Many supposedly committed Christians are accepting counterfeit experiences and "miracles," and are involving themselves in beliefs and practices that are not only unscriptural, but also originate in the occult and Eastern mysticism.

It's understandable when non-Christians who have blinded minds (2 Corinthians 4:4) and lack spiritual discernment (1 Corinthians 2:14) participate in such things, but when professing Christians become involved in this deception, especially Christian leaders who should know God's Word and have discernment, it is cause for concern. Jesus showed compassion to the masses and to those enslaved in sin, but was very strong in rebuking the scribes and the Pharisees who should have had spiritual discernment.

I Have Nothing to Gain

I have nothing to gain from writing a book like this. I make no personal profit from it. If I gain anything, it is increased opposition, spiritual warfare, and a possible loss of financial support. But I must be obedient to the Lord no matter the cost.

I can identify with Jeremiah who said:

O LORD, thou hast deceived me, and I was deceived; thou art stronger than I, and hast prevailed: I am in derision daily, every one mocketh me. For since I spake, I cried out, I cried violence and spoil; because the word of the LORD was made a reproach unto me, and a derision, daily. Then I said, I will not make mention of him, nor speak any more in his name. But his word was in mine heart as a burning fire shut up in my bones, and I was weary with forbearing, and I could not stay. For I heard the defaming of many, fear on every side. Report, say they, and we will report it. All my familiars watched for my halting, saying, Peradventure he will be enticed, and we shall prevail against him, and we shall take our revenge on him. But the LORD is with me as a mighty terrible one: therefore my persecutors shall stumble, and they shall not prevail: they shall be greatly ashamed; for they shall not prosper: their everlasting confusion shall never be forgotten. (Jeremiah 20:7–11)

Building His Church

Before becoming a Christian, I had a great interest in Eastern religion, the occult, and New Age beliefs and practices. Afterwards,

I researched and exposed them for almost twenty years. Now it is sad indeed to see supposed brothers and sisters in Christ embrace beliefs and practices out of which the Lord rescued me.

The focus of my ministry is to emphasize what I stand for (biblical Christianity), not what I am against. However, some people are so comfortable with the counterfeit that they reject the real thing. So, the false must be exposed and removed if people are to understand and accept genuine biblical Christianity.

If a foundation is laid other than Christ, we must remove it before we can build on Christ—the true foundation of the Church. If someone began building on the foundation of Christ but has fallen into beliefs or techniques contrary to Scripture, we must tear out the defective materials and replace them with materials of good quality.

Jeremiah 1:10 states: "See, I have this day set thee over the nations and over the kingdoms, to root out, and to pull down, and to destroy, and to throw down, to build, and to plant."

Deception in the Last Days

The main descriptive word of the last days is deception. Jesus warns about false prophets and false christs in Matthew 24:5, 11, and 24. In 2 Thessalonians 2:3, 9–12, Paul cautions against "the apostasy and signs and false wonders." In 1 Timothy 4:1, he warns about "deceitful spirits and doctrines of demons." In 2 Timothy 4:3–4, Paul reveals that there will be those who "will not endure sound doctrine; but after their own lusts shall they heap to themselves teachers, having itching ears; And they shall turn away their ears from the truth, and shall be turned unto fables." In Revelation 13:13, 14, and 19:20, John informs his readers that the inhabitants of the earth will be deceived because of the signs that the false prophet performs in the presence of the Antichrist. The seduction of that deception will be so insidious in the last days, Jesus cautioned in Matthew 24:24, that if it were possible, even the elect would be deceived.

I see the elect, or those who profess to be the elect, involved in teachings, practices, and techniques of which the roots are Eastern and the occult. People are blindly accepting these false teachings that are erroneously defended by Scriptures quoted out of context. To these misguided Christians, it appears that Jesus Christ is being praised and exalted, and that benefits do result (albeit temporarily).

Today, while atheists and liberal theologians seek to undermine the authority of Scripture and redefine the Jesus of the Bible, many so-called committed Christians are allowing "new revelations" and "new teachings" that go beyond the Word of God to do likewise.

Your Praise is Empty and Meaningless

You can praise and exalt the Lord all you want with your mouth and raise your hands to worship Him, but if you are involved in phenomena and practices that are New Age in nature, your praise is empty and meaningless, and you have lost your discernment.

Isaiah 29:13, 14 warns: "Wherefore the Lord said, Forasmuch as this people draw near me with their mouth, and with their lips do honour me, but have removed their heart far from me, and their fear toward me is taught by the precept of men: Therefore, behold, I will proceed to do a marvellous work among this people, even a marvellous work and a wonder: for the wisdom of their wise men shall perish, and the understanding of their prudent men shall be hid."

They say they are free in the Spirit, but they are in reality bound to the teachings of men. They have become clones of those who have indoctrinated them in the current trends and phenomena. This results in worship, dance, testimonies, prophecies, and experiences that are an imitation of this conditioning. Jesus, quoting the prophet Isaiah, rebuked the religious leaders: "He answered and said unto them, Well hath Esaias prophesied of you hypocrites, as it is written, This people honoureth me with their lips, but their heart is far from me" (Mark 7:6).

Witchcraft in the Church?

Many years ago, I warned about witchcraft infiltrating churches and seducing away immature Christians. In a newsletter article entitled, "Witchcraft Infiltrates Churches," I revealed how several Christians had gotten involved with a woman who was involved in witchcraft and spiritualism.

The strategy of this woman, who professed to be a born-again, Spirit-filled Christian, was to infiltrate a church or ministry. She would quote extensively from Scripture, enabling her to subtly seduce immature Christians into occult philosophy and practices.

Far more subtle and harmful, however, is the fact that today many Christian leaders, obviously lacking Scriptural knowledge and discernment, and *ignorant* of the occult and Eastern mysticism, are now the main ones bringing it into the Church.

Why All the Deception?

Before we examine some of these beliefs, practices, and techniques, here are a few reasons why deception is so rampant in the body of Christ today:

1) There is an obvious lack of consistent and intense Bible study and discernment by many Christians and Christian leaders.

2) Scripture has been twisted to portray love and unity as the highest goal of the Church. This extremism calls for unity at the *cost* of doctrinal purity.

3) The out-of-context and biblically unbalanced concept of "do not judge" makes it impossible to be a Berean (one who measures all things by the Scriptures).

4) There is a new and insatiable quest for more exciting spiritual experiences and "new revelations." Many are allowing subjective feelings to determine their beliefs, rather than evaluating all spiritual experiences, "prophecies," and "new revelations" by the objective Word of God.

5) Many Christian leaders are unknowingly teaching beliefs and techniques that are New Age, Eastern, and occult in nature. They have learned them at seminars, conferences, conventions, and through reading so-called "Christian" books.

6) Some pastors are aware of the New Age and Eastern overtones in such practices as yoga and the martial arts but indifferently allow them in the church.

7) Other supposed Christians and Christian leaders, I am convinced, who have an agenda based on New Age and occult beliefs and practices, have infiltrated the Church and are subtly seeking to indoctrinate the body of Christ.

Every Christian, and especially every Christian leader, has a responsibility to test all practices, revelations, and teachings by Scripture, and not merely to accept and propagate them because they are popular. If they would do this, they would see how these teachings are plainly contrary to God's Word and Spirit.

Chapter Two

HOW FAR DO WE GO WITH "LOVE AND UNITY" AND "DO NOT JUDGE"?

The Lord knows the Church needs more love and unity (John 17:22, 23; Ephesians 4:13; Philippians 2:2). There is far too much backbiting, gossiping, division, and dissension. Church splits occur over the most ridiculous irrelevancies. We need to be unified in the true faith to guard against those who, in pride and lacking genuine love, take a strong stance on many non-crucial issues, causing needless harm to the body of Christ.

I will not, however, for the sake of love and unity, unite with those who propagate false doctrine that corrupts the foundation of biblical Christianity. I will not involve myself in techniques and practices that I know to be of the occult or counterfeit, thus uniting with the very spirit of antichrist.

The God of the Bible who has been so faithful in my life,

and who has supernaturally protected me and spared my life on numerous occasions, has not done so for me to proclaim an unscriptural message of compromise. I am compelled by His Word and Spirit to accurately and boldly proclaim His truth in love. And that is exactly what I intend to do until I go home to be with Him or until He returns.

I refuse to compromise my commitment to Christ and His Word for the sake of man-made love and unity. God will have no more part of that than He did with the Tower of Babel, which He exposed as nothing but unified rebellion.

If God is a God who advocates love and unity at all costs, as some would have us believe, then why did He stop the building of the Tower of Babel? Why did He command Israel to maintain her separation from all the idolatry, occultism, and paganism going on around her? Why did He tell Moses to be sure His people made no covenant with the inhabitants of the land they were to possess (Exodus 34:12–16)? Why did He rebuke righteous King Jehoshaphat of Judah and destroy his ships for making an alliance with wicked King Ahaziah of Israel (2 Chronicles 20:35–37)? Why did Zerubbabel and Jeshua refuse to allow their enemies (even though they said, "We, like you, seek your God; and we have been sacrificing to Him") to have any part in helping them rebuild the temple but responded to them, "You have nothing in common with us" (Ezra 4:1–3)? Why did the Apostle John tell us not to receive into our house or even give a greeting to anyone who does not bring the true Gospel message (2 John 7–11)? Why did God tell His people to come out of Babylon the Great so as not to participate in her sins and receive of her plagues (Revelation 18:1–4)?

The Bible speaks of a new age of love, unity, peace, and prosperity after Christ returns to this earth to rule and reign. It repeatedly warns, however, that before the true millennium on Earth and the new heavens and new earth, there will be a period of unprecedented false unity on a worldwide level culminating in unified worship, political power, and economic control. This occult-empowered system of delusion and oppression is referred to as *Mystery Babylon.*

The current false unity movement is rapidly moving toward merging apostate Christianity and New Ageism to achieve its ultimate goals of global unity, peace, and prosperity—without submission and obedience to the true Creator. These goals include such humanly appealing concepts as a worldwide celebration of joy, the achieving of individual godhood, cleansing the earth of all *evil,* and the establishing of *God's* kingdom.

What appears on the surface to the undiscerning as a Christ-centered movement is in reality a satanically-inspired and demonically-driven movement. Revelation 13:8 gives the ultimate end of this counterfeit love and unity: "And all that dwell upon the earth shall worship him [the Antichrist], whose names are not written in the book of life of the Lamb slain from the foundation of the world."

Just Who IS Causing Division?

Many are quick to quote Romans 16:17 (out of context) about keeping away from those who cause division, but they conveniently leave out an important part of that verse. The total verse reads: "Now I beseech you, brethren, mark them which cause divisions and offenses contrary to the doctrine which ye have learned; and avoid them."

Therefore, the ones we are to *mark* and *avoid* are not those who are causing division while standing for the truth, but we are to *mark* and *avoid* those who cause division because they are luring people away from the truth.

Who is causing the real divisions in the body of Christ? Not those who are standing in love and biblical accuracy, who rebuke and correct those in error. Rather it is those who allow this New Age, occult-driven, antichrist spirit to infiltrate the Church.

Paul encouraged the Philippians to "Only let your conversation be as it becometh the gospel of Christ: that whether I come and see you, or else be absent, I may hear of your affairs, that ye stand fast in one spirit, with one mind striving together for the faith of the gospel; And in nothing terrified by your adversaries: which is to them an evident token of perdition, but to you of salvation, and that of God" (Philippians 1:27, 28).

Contend Earnestly for the Faith

In Philippians 1:17, Paul says, "...I am set for the defence of the Gospel." Jude 3 admonishes us to "exhort you that ye should earnestly contend for the faith which was once delivered unto the saints."

The faith that I am proclaiming today is the same faith I have been proclaiming since giving my life to Christ in 1971. I have learned, adapted, and changed a few things here and there, but my basic message of biblical Christianity stands firm. I am teaching the same biblical principles God taught me through His Word and Spirit many years ago. These principles have proven far superior than Eastern, occult, and New Age beliefs and techniques in enabling a person to reach their maximum potential in Christ.

No, I have not changed. These supposed brothers and sisters

have changed. They have turned aside to the right or to the left (Deuteronomy 28:14; Joshua 1:7; 2 Kings 22:2) and forsaken their pure devotion to Christ and His Word. They have accepted new teachings, new phenomena, "new revelations," and "new truth"—which go beyond and are contrary to the Word of God. They have involved themselves in groups, movements, beliefs, and practices that have compromised their commitment to biblical Christianity and brought an unholy mixture into the Church ("the cup of the Lord and the cup of demons"—1 Corinthians 10:21). Many of them are, in reality, now proclaiming "another Jesus, another gospel, and another spirit"—and multitudes who don't know God's Word and have discernment are getting caught up in it.

Paul writes to the Galatians, "Ye did run well; who did hinder you that ye should not obey the truth? This persuasion cometh not of him that calleth you. A little leaven leaveneth the whole lump" (Galatians 5:7–9).

1 John 2:18, 19 admonishes, "Little children, it is the last time: and as ye have heard that antichrist shall come, even now are there many antichrists; whereby we know that it is the last time. They went out from us, but they were not of us; for if they had been of us, they would no doubt have continued with us: but they went out, that they might be made manifest that they were not all of us."

2 John 7–11 warns, "For many deceivers are entered into the world, who confess not that Jesus Christ is come in the flesh. This is a deceiver and an antichrist. Look to yourselves, that we lose not those things which we have wrought, but that we receive a full reward. Whosoever transgresseth, and abideth not in the doctrine of Christ, hath not God. He that abideth in the doctrine of Christ, he hath both the Father and the Son. If there come any

unto you, and bring not this doctrine, receive him not into your house, neither bid him God speed: For he that biddeth him God speed is partaker of his evil deeds."

In the early days of my ministry, I rubbed shoulders with many Christian leaders, about whom I was uncertain. Their message wasn't blatantly unscriptural, but their experiences and beliefs caused me to wonder. I knew in my spirit that something was wrong; I just wasn't quite sure what it was. Years later as I matured in Christ and the knowledge of His Word, and as they progressed down the path of compromise, their teachings and techniques became visibly unbiblical. I realized why I had had *skirmishes* with these people years earlier.

Will the Real Christianity Please Stand Up?

Today we are seeing biblical Christianity (the faith which was once for all delivered to the saints by God's Word) being replaced by what I call "New Age Christianity." A whole new Christianity is being developed by those who embrace New Age philosophies and practices. They think it is the outpouring of God's Spirit— renewal, restoration, and revival. It is, however, the fulfillment of biblical prophecy concerning apostasy and deception that Jesus, Paul, John, and Peter warned about and foretold would permeate the generation immediately preceding Christ's return.

The unity many are seeking to establish is not a unity based upon biblical truth. It is a unity built on tolerance of anything and everything, an agreement not to disagree, and based on subjective experiences.

While many "Christian" leaders distance themselves from biblical Christians for being too "divisive," they seemingly have no problem cozying up to those who propagate unbiblical beliefs and practices. Equally offensive are those who knowingly tolerate error so they can have financial gain, popularity, success, and power.

Unity at the expense of truth is apostasy. Israel's attempt to serve both Yahweh and Baal resulted in God's punishment. So, too, the Church's unholy mix and spiritual adultery will eventually lead to God's judgment.

It is amazing how those who supposedly advocate love and unity become so unloving, vengeful, and divisive when opposed, exposed, or Scripturally corrected. Some "Christians" are becoming *spiritual terrorists* by refusing to deal face-to-face with Scriptural issues. Instead they covertly whisper, mutter, undermine, and twist the truth. Their surface appearance of love and being non-judgmental quickly degenerates into hostility and verbal backstabbing.

Do Not Judge

While I was speaking to one of many such groups, the Lord strongly urged me to speak out against some of the false teachings they endorsed. At the conclusion I gave the following invitation to everyone: "If you have a disagreement, or if anything I have said is unscriptural, now is your opportunity to correct me publicly." No one spoke.

I even told the leader I would be happy to meet with any pastor or representative from her group to Scripturally evaluate these issues. Again, there was no response.

While several did respond to the altar call and repented, the leader and some of the others who refused to do so—those who are so much against "judging" and so much in favor of "love and unity"—cowardly retaliated behind my back, attempting to discredit what I had said.

When the leader was later confronted by a member of the group, who reminded her of my public challenge, the leader made an excuse that she didn't hear everything I said because for much of the time she had been "praying in the Spirit." This is also unscriptural, because Scripture teaches us to examine all things carefully. I have seen Hare Krishna devotees do something similar when I tried to share the evidence and uniqueness of Jesus Christ with them. But never a biblical Christian! This Christian leader was wrongly using "praying in the Spirit" in the same blocking manner as the Krishnas would use their chanting.

Ironically, these leaders, who after much prayer had concluded that the Lord directed them to ask me to speak, did not feel led of the Lord to accept the message He sent me to proclaim!

When I speak to such groups, it reminds me of Stephen (Acts 7:1–60) or Paul (Acts 22:1–23) who made their defense to the Jewish leaders. As long as they were reviewing the way God dealt with the Jews in the Old Testament or conveying their salvation experience, the Jewish leaders remained civil, because they were hearing what they wanted to hear. But, when Stephen or Paul gave them words of correction from the Holy Spirit and the Scriptures, or said something that offended them, they became extremely hostile and wanted to kill them (Acts 7:51–54; 22:21–23).

So, too, when I share my testimony and some of the many miracles the Lord has done, they love it and listen intently, but if I give a word of caution or warning concerning all the New Age and occult techniques and beliefs that are infiltrating the Church or their need to repent of spiritual adultery, their countenance changes. An expression of hostility comes onto many of their faces. The atmosphere gets tense as they resist, stiffen their necks, and harden their hearts.

Allow me to point out a Scriptural distinction here. When we are dealing with a personal problem between two Christians, or someone in sin, we should attempt to deal with it privately. If he does not receive it, then take one or two witnesses and in their presence confront him again, but if that person still refuses to listen, then we are to take it publicly before the church (Matthew 18:15–17).

On the other hand, there are numerous Scriptural accounts of dealing with error and false teachings that should be dealt with publicly, since they are being openly proclaimed.

Beware of Wolves Dressed in Sheep's Clothing

To those of you who would say, "Judge not," let me remind you that every time you speak out against abortion, pornography, child molestation, animal abuse, drugs and alcohol, politics, sorcery, and so on, you are "judging." In order to be wise and discerning, one must make sound judgments. So be consistent, and not hypocritical in your treatment of this subject.

The phrase "do not judge" used in Matthew 7:1–5 is being twisted, misinterpreted, and taken out of context. As a result, it is creating a dangerous environment that discourages biblical discernment.

Yet in this very chapter it tells us to "Beware of the false prophets, who come to you in sheep's clothing, but inwardly are ravenous wolves" (Matthew 7:15). How can I identify wolves in sheep's clothing unless I use discernment and "judge" their doctrine and fruit? How can we beware unless we evaluate them in accordance with God's Word?

If a "sheep" comes into the flock and begins biting, chewing, eating, and killing the other sheep, it doesn't take much discernment to know this creature is not a sheep, but a wolf in sheep's clothing. Many false teachers conceal themselves behind the smoke screen of "do not judge," causing many believers and their shepherds to feel guilty about their God-ordained duty to discern.

I have cautioned many pastors who were opening their churches to people and groups bringing in "new" teachings and practices in an attempt to generate spiritual renewal, excitement, and growth in their congregations. Almost every pastor who ignored the warning and proceeded had some initial gain but great long term loss. Within months or years their flocks were fleeced and the church was either split or taken over. Several of these pastors had to move on to new churches—some left the ministry altogether. All because in their desire for growth and excitement they tolerated and accepted nonbiblical teachings and practices.

Have You Been Spiritually Violated?

We are appalled at news accounts of people who sit idly by watching someone on the street being raped or murdered without intervening, yet that same mentality has infiltrated the Church. What this unbiblical attitude is really saying is: "Don't confront people when they are in error. Don't stand up for the truth. Don't biblically evaluate teachings and practices. Don't be a Berean. Don't follow the example of Jesus and Paul and other New Testament writers. Don't expose error. Don't contend earnestly for the faith. Just flow along in the spirit of love, unity, convenience, compromise, and conformity."

People are being spiritually raped today, and anyone who attempts to intervene or Scripturally deal with the issues is labeled as unloving, gossiping, judging, attacking, witch-hunting, holding an inquisition, being negative, divisive, hurting the Body, being a Pharisee, being self-righteous, and the like. This mentality in the Church today is really a spirit of fear, cowardice, and compromise. As a result, shepherds stand idly by while the wolves ravage the unsuspecting flock or indifferently tolerate unbiblical practices in their church.

Woe to you false shepherds who lead God's sheep astray, for one day you will stand before God to give an account for your compromising and cowardly behavior!

Who Really Troubles the Body?

"New Age Christian" leaders imply that those who are exposing error in the Church, who are standing uncompromisingly and boldly for biblical truth, and who are refusing to unite with their false teachings are "troubling the Body." Their attitude reminds me of King Ahab whose sin brought judgment on Israel. When he saw Elijah, he asked accusingly, "Art thou he that troubleth Israel?" (1 Kings 18:17). Elijah responded, "I have not troubled Israel; but thou, and thy father's house, in that ye have forsaken the commandments of the LORD, and thou hast followed Baalim" (1 Kings 18:18).

I will not stand by as people are being spiritually raped, just as I would not stand by if your wife or your child was being raped or molested on the street. I would risk my life to save them as I have done before on numerous occasions when I intervened to help someone.

By God's grace I will stand in integrity and commitment to the God of the Bible and intervene by boldly speaking out when I see people being spiritually raped.

Why Beware?

The motivation for writing *Beware*, the book you are now reading (first compiled in a condensed booklet version in 1989), came as a result of responding to a pastor who spiritually raped many unsuspecting people during his ministry. Initially, almost fifty of his victims came to me for help concerning occult and New Age teachings and practices he had led them into. Many more have come forward over the years. They were deeply hurt and confused. Several were no longer even walking with the Lord. Fortunately, many of them are now growing in Christ in churches where genuine biblical Christianity is being proclaimed.

In obedience to the Lord and after much prayer and fasting, I confronted this pastor alone—with restoration as my goal. Then I took two witnesses. But when he still refused to repent and would not meet with his victims to Scripturally deal with these issues, the Lord strongly impressed on my heart to write *Beware*.

Little did I know when I first wrote the booklet in 1989, that it would impact countless lives around the world. I thought I was merely dealing with a local situation, but quickly discovered these same teachings and phenomena were affecting churches and ministries worldwide. The Lord later showed me that confronting this pastor was really the secondary issue. He was merely using that as motivation for the writing of *Beware*, which has proven to be both a warning and a great help and blessing to countless believers and leaders in the body of Christ throughout the world.

The person who motivated the writing of the *Beware* booklet tried to dig up anything to discredit me and my ministry. He even contacted the pastor of the church I attended and those in leadership in the movement with whom I was credentialed. When he found nothing on me, he spread lies to divert attention from the real issues. But the Lord gave me Psalm 37 (especially verses 1–13 and 32–34), where it speaks of waiting patiently and resting in Him because He will eventually bless those who trust in Him, but the wicked will wither like grass and be no more.

I know why this pastor refused to deal with these issues before the Church; he knew that the teachings and techniques he was propagating were not only impossible to defend from Scripture, but were occult practices and New Age in nature. So, like a child molester or rapist attempting to conceal a double life, this pastor attempted to hide behind a facade of legitimate Christianity. Instead of repenting, he used the "new revelations" and false prophecies of so-called prophets and apostles to give him opportunities to seduce and spiritually rape many more unsuspecting victims. Years later he fled his church in a self-induced scandal that rocked even his ardent followers.

When I initially wrote my *Beware* booklet in 1989, I indicated that these false teachings and unbiblical phenomena would escalate in the Church. Unfortunately, this escalation of spiritual deception has proven to be accurate.

Warn God's People

God is adamant throughout the Scriptures in His opposition toward those who lead His people astray. The responsibility of Christian leaders to be Scripturally sound is of the utmost importance. Their eternal destiny, and that of their flocks, depends on it.

In Deuteronomy 13, for example, God calls for the death penalty to be administered to anyone who would lure away the people of God into following after other gods—even if the sign or wonder they gave came to pass. Rebellion against God's Law was punished. If God would go to that extreme in the Old Testament, don't you think He at least wants us today to stand up and challenge "Christian leaders" who are misguiding God's people and enticing them into beliefs and techniques that are New Age and of the occult? We must warn God's people, for they are being drawn away from pure devotion to Him.

As a teenager, I remember many guys who were so brave and tough when they were with their friends, but were wimps when they were alone. This is also true for many ministers and Christians who are twisting and perverting God's Word. They are so brave and bold and confident when they are with their "support groups," but so cowardly when alone. Although these people are publicly proclaiming their false teachings because they are popular, when challenged to Scripturally deal with the issues, they are unwilling to do so. They know they cannot defend their unscriptural beliefs and involvements.

Jesus, Paul, and Others Spoke Out

Many books of the New Testament were written to expose false teachings and to encourage believers to obey and preserve sound doctrine.

Jesus, the Apostles Paul and John, and other New Testament writers repeatedly warned the people of God to beware of false prophets, teachers, and messiahs. They were not afraid to publicly speak out against them using biting rebukes and names, such as: "You brood of vipers" (Matthew 3:7; 12:34); "hypocrites," "whitewashed tombs" (Matthew 23:27); "dogs," "evil workers" (Philippians 3:2). Hymenaeus and Alexander are mentioned by name: "whom I have delivered over to Satan, so that they may be taught not to blaspheme" (1 Timothy 1:18–20). Hymenaeus and Philetus are exposed specifically as "men whom have gone astray from the truth" (2 Timothy 2:17, 18). Of Demas it is said, "having loved this present world, [he] has deserted me" (2 Timothy 4:10); of Alexander the coppersmith, "[he] did me much harm" (2 Timothy 4:14, 15); and of Diotrephes, "who loves to be first and unjustly accuses us with wicked words" (3 John 9, 10).

Today's wolves in sheep's clothing cry out that public debate and exposure will hurt new Christians. Apollos, however, "mightily convinced the Jews, and that publicly, shewing by the scriptures that Jesus was Christ" (Acts 18:28). It did not hurt anyone but the deceivers, for it is written, "[he] who, when he was come, helped them much which had believed through grace" (Acts 18:27). As Charles Spurgeon has (and others have) written, "Darkness hates the light."

The only ones who may be "hurt" are those who have built their lives on the false prophets and phenomena instead of on the Lord and His Word. Hopefully it will "hurt" them enough to drive them to their knees to seek the Lord with all their hearts, and motivate them to get into His Word to "rightly divide the Word of Truth," and walk in the genuine power of His Spirit.

Paul confronted Peter to his face (Galatians 2:11) for his compromising spirit and he did so publicly, before them all (Galatians 2:14).

In 1 Corinthians 5:12, 13 Paul states, "For what have I to do to judge them also that are without? do not ye judge them that are within? But them that are without God judgeth. Therefore put away from among yourselves that wicked person."

Paul told Timothy, "Against an elder receive not an accusation, but before two or three witnesses. Them that sin rebuke before all, that others also may fear" (1 Timothy 5:19, 20).

Paul says in Galatians 6:1, "Brethren, if a man be overtaken in a fault, ye which are spiritual, restore such an one in the spirit of meekness; considering thyself, lest thou also be tempted."

It's Time to Stand for the Truth

A well-known Scripture on love is 1 Corinthians 13. But there are more. Proverbs 3:12 says, "For whom the LORD loveth he correcteth…" 1 John 2:5 states, "But whoso keepeth his word, in him verily is the love of God perfected…" 2 John 6 declares, "And this is love, that we walk after his commandments…" And Jesus said in John 14:15, "If ye love me, keep my commandments."

We are living in a day and age when we must stand up not only with love, but also with courage and boldness to confront, expose, and seek to Scripturally correct error. I have had to stand alone on many occasions against cultists, occultists, New Agers, and even supposed Christians who have distorted God's Word.

Jeremiah 1:17–19 encourages, "Thou therefore gird up thy loins, and arise, and speak unto them all that I command thee: be not dismayed at their faces, lest I confound thee before them. For, behold, I have made thee this day a defenced city, and an iron pillar, and brasen walls against the whole land, against the kings of Judah, against the princes thereof, against the priests thereof, and against the people of the land. And they shall fight against thee; but they shall not prevail against thee; for I am with thee, saith the LORD, to deliver thee."

Over the years the Lord has led me to speak out in love concerning several teachings and groups. This resulted in much temporary uproar and opposition because many were initially convinced I was totally wrong and out of line. In time, however, the Lord always vindicated me. Sometimes it was only a matter of weeks. Other times it took years, but the Lord has always been faithful, and the end result has been victory.

The difficulties, opposition, and spiritual warfare incurred have been worth it. Many of those involved in these various teachings and groups have eventually called, written, or come by the ministry center to inform me they have repented before the Lord, discontinued their involvement, and have renewed their desire to totally live for the Christ of the Bible and biblical Christianity.

A Scriptural Perspective

People frequently ask my opinion about various pastors or churches. Although it is Scripturally justifiable, I generally try not to take a position on a person or church, or mention names. Instead, I try to take a stance on teachings and techniques after evaluating them biblically. Then I seek to present a Scriptural perspective. That is what we are going to do throughout the rest of this book.

Chapter Three

ARE PSYCHOSPIRITUAL
TECHNIQUES BIBLICAL?

Inner Healing, Visualization, Imaging...

Psychospiritual techniques are replacing the genuine transforming power of the Holy Spirit in many Christians' lives.
Many supposed believers in Christ are accepting these
counterfeit and inferior spiritual experiences instead of choosing
to walk in obedience to God's Word and knowing the genuine
power of His Holy Spirit.

Many don't want to hear about repentance, commitment,
obedience, discipline, and self-control. These biblical principles
of spiritual growth are not quick and easy. They take time, effort,
and dedication—and there is a cost.

Therefore, many look to some psychospiritual, New Age,
or Eastern technique and try to Christianize it. But you can't
Christianize these techniques. They are contrary to Scripture and
rooted in occultism.

God's way is far superior. I have obtained greater physical, emotional, and spiritual health through applying biblical principles than I ever did through any other means.

How Dangerous is the New Age?

In an article entitled, "Escaping the New Age," by Paul McGuire, his answer to the question, "How dangerous is the New Age?" was: "There are two great dangers. One is New Age thinking infiltrating the Christian church through things such as relaxation exercises, visualization, imaginary Jesus's, various forms of mind control, meditation and stress management. You see a lot of these things taught in Christian churches and much of it is occult influenced or Eastern mysticism-based… An equal danger is an over reactionary paranoia in the Christian culture where something is called New Age when it isn't."[1]

Imagery and Visualization

What some people call imaging and visualization is nothing more than mentally picturing biblical accounts. What some people call inner healing is merely praying for forgiveness and healing of past hurts. What some people call meditation is nothing more than concentration and focusing one's attention on the principle or skill being taught. And what some people call hypnosis is just relaxation or reinforcing Scripture. These are, for the most part, harmless-but-unadvised uses of New Age jargon.

Imaging and visualization in the true sense is the technique of actively forming a mental picture in the mind, with the intent of changing the material world or the spiritual realm. This technique is used extensively, but not exclusively, in the inner healing ministry. For example, one is first instructed to image or visualize a scene, a situation, a person, or a confrontation, and then to imagine Jesus entering the picture, where the scene is reenacted with Jesus now healing all the particular scars incurred during that incident. One grave danger is that the Jesus imaged is not said to be an image, but the real Jesus, actually dialoguing with the person.

Johanna Michaelsen, who was deeply involved in the occult, but is now a Christian, states in her book, *Like Lambs to the Slaughter:* "There are perfectly valid and legitimate uses of the imagination… An artist 'sees' the finished painting or sculpture in his mind or an architect 'visualizes' the building he is working on… When we recall past events in our lives, we do so with mental images. Listening to a storyteller or reading a book can produce vivid mental images. When I studied theater, I mentally rehearsed my roles. Such envisioning is not what I'm talking about. What I'm talking about is a technique of creating an image in your mind and using that image in an *effort to create or control reality through mind-powers.*"[2]

Entering the Realm of Sorcery

Many who practice guided imagery and visualization do subtle Scripture changes. For example, Romans 8:29, which speaks of "being changed into the image of Jesus," is twisted to "being changed into the Jesus we image."

While I am all for mentally rehearsing Scripture and using imagination for biblical accounts, I am against attempting to create physical or spiritual reality, or to cause mystical experiences through any mind technique. Any time you attempt to change, alter, or create reality, you are then entering the realm of sorcery.

When those who practice imagery and visualization believe that the Jesus being imaged in their minds is not just an image, but the real Jesus (even going so far as to dialogue and touch Him), then they have opened the door to counterfeit spirit guides.

You may think you are praying to the God of the Bible. Your motive might be right, but if your method is wrong, it can open you up to deception and familiar spirits.

You should never attempt to visualize or conjure Jesus or God the Father in the room with you as you pray. This opens your mind to a false entity, that is a product of your imagination or an evil spirit disguising itself as the Holy Spirit, Jesus, God the Father, or an angelic being.

You might think you're focusing on Jesus. You might have a real spiritual experience. But, when you create Jesus in your mind, He is not the historic Jesus of the Bible. He is YOUR experience of that Jesus. The Bible warns about "another Jesus." Many, through these techniques, have testified that the Jesus they encountered was not the resurrected Christ, but another Jesus, a counterfeit, "the angel of light" impersonating the Jesus of the Bible.

Long before it became a popular practice in Christian circles, Napoleon Hill wrote about imagery and visualization in his book, *Think and Grow Rich.* He writes:

The THIRTEENTH principle is known as the sixth sense, through which Infinite Intelligence may and will communicate voluntarily, without any effort from, or demands by, the individual… Step by step, through the preceding chapters, you have been led to this, the last principle. If you have mastered each of the preceding principles, you are now prepared to accept, *without being skeptical,* the stupendous claims made here...

Just before going to sleep at night, I would shut my eyes, and see, in my imagination, this group of men seated with me around my council table...

After some months of this nightly procedure, I was astounded by the discovery that these imaginary figures became apparently real.

Each of these nine men developed individual characteristics, which surprised me...

These meetings became so realistic that I became fearful of their consequences, and discontinued them for several months. The experiences were so uncanny, I was afraid if I continued them I would lose sight of the fact that the meetings were purely *experiences of my imagination.*[3]

In an article in the *New Age Journal* on "The Healing Power of Imagery," a medical doctor shares many of the supposed benefits of imagery and visualization, but reveals that this New Age healing method is in reality "Old Age" occultism because you are encouraged to contact your inner advisor. He states:

After you've gotten comfortable with your imagery, you may want to explore it further, searching for new ways to support your self-healing. You may want to meet your inner advisor... Whatever you believe—that the adviser is a spirit, a guardian angel, a messenger from God, a hallucination, a communication from your right brain to your left, or a symbolic representation of inner wisdom—is all right. The fact is, no one knows what it is with any certainty. We can each decide for ourselves...

Sometimes people will encounter religious figures like Jesus, Moses, or Buddha, while others will find an angel, fairy, or leprechaun. People sometimes encounter the advisor as a light or a translucent spirit... The best way to work with this and any other imagery experience is just to let the figures be whatever they are. Welcome the advisor that comes and get to know it as it is.[4]

You're Not Imaging the Real Jesus

A woman having problems with fear was introduced to visualization and inner healing by a friend. They started with prayer as they held hands facing each other. Then the woman was told to visualize Jesus on the cross, but all she could visualize was the bottom of the cross and his legs. She quickly realized they were not the legs of Jesus, but those of her deceased father. So she was told to visualize a past traumatic experience with her father and picture Jesus in her mind there with her.

She got to the place where she was able to visualize Jesus, but he was at a distance and she wasn't able to see his face clearly because he was wearing a hood that was attached to his robe. She was told to visualize him closer. As she did, he immediately became so close she could only see the white garments on his chest.

She then was told to wrap her arms around this Jesus. She just couldn't bring herself to do so, although that was what she really wanted. She was told to picture Jesus putting his arms around her and to feel his love. Then she felt a sensation and awareness that his arms were around her, but she still couldn't bring herself to put her arms around him. Getting frustrated and not knowing why she couldn't put her arms around Jesus, they ended the session.

For the following two weeks, she was upset with herself and was seeking the Lord as to why she couldn't put her arms around "Jesus," until God strongly spoke to her heart, "That wasn't Jesus!" Then she knew it was demonic. She now thanks God for His protection in her ignorance and seeks to know the real Jesus with all her heart through His Word and Spirit.

The Dangers of Inner Healing

Inner healing refers to the healing of one's memories and hurts from the past, whether known or unknown. Inner healing involves visual reconstruction of a past traumatic experience and then visualizing Jesus supposedly entering the situation, bringing His healing, love, comfort, and forgiveness.

Although we can all agree that God wants us to heal our hurts, bitterness, hate, and resentment, it is the *technique or method* used to obtain inner healing that we must consider. Such techniques as centering, imagery, and visualization are indeed potentially dangerous spiritually.

Consider the individual sent by her pastor for inner healing. The inner healers supposedly regressed the girl back to her mother's womb, and along with other lies, told her that her mother and father didn't want her. The next day the girl's eyes were swollen shut from crying. Not only can these experiences be potentially dangerous spiritually, but they can be emotionally damaging as well.

The "garbage" and "stench" of our past does not need to be dwelled on. It needs to be forgiven, crucified, and buried. Philippians 3:13, 14 says, "Brethren, I count not myself to have apprehended: but this one thing I do, forgetting those things which are behind, and reaching forth unto those things which are before, I press toward the mark for the prize of the high calling of God in Christ Jesus."

After I spoke at a Christian women's group, the president of the group told me how her "Christian" doctor, who is promoting holistic health, took her through a regression process during an inner healing session.

At first she told me it made her feel wonderful and helped her so much. As I questioned her, she informed me this supposed Christian doctor was also into yin and yang, along with Eastern and occult philosophies and techniques.

When I told her that she had submitted her mind to an occultist and involved herself in a New Age and occult technique, she recalled that she did think it strange that during this inner healing process the first words that entered her mind were "Jesus Christ, you S.O.B!" She immediately renounced her involvement, and God gave her genuine peace and joy.

Most Christians Don't Understand Occultism

If you had come to one of the soccer games I coached and saw the referee call "hands" or "offside" or give a team a "penalty kick," you would be confused if you didn't know the basic rules of soccer. But once you understand the rules of soccer, you can identify what's happening on the field.

So, too, if you understand basic occultism and Eastern mysticism, you can easily identify it when you begin to see it manifest in the Church. Yet, many Christian leaders who have little or no understanding of the occult, Eastern mysticism, and the New Age, ignorantly accept and propagate those beliefs and techniques.

Interestingly, while many researchers, as well as former occultists and New Agers who have become committed Christians, are speaking out against these activities, many Christian leaders who do not have a basic understanding of the source and origin of these techniques and beliefs are endorsing them.

Don Matzat, a long-time leader in the charismatic renewal, wrote a book entitled, *Inner Healing: Deliverance or Deception?* After thoroughly researching his subject, Matzat points out four basic truths about inner healing: (1) inner healing is not based upon Scripture, but upon the psychological theories of atheist Sigmund Freud and occultist Carl Jung; (2) inner healing is contrary to the clear teachings of Scripture; (3) inner healing is not based on scientific truth, but theories of the subconscious mind; and (4) visualization, an element in inner healing, has nothing whatever to do with Christianity, but is an occult technique for reaching spirit guides.

The Deception of Centering (Meditation)

Centering, a euphemism for meditation, is the act of willfully moving oneself into a passive mental state by putting all thoughts to rest. This practice may or may not involve breathing exercises and relaxation techniques. Centering (though it may not be labeled as such) is often used in Christian circles in order to engage in visualization.

One former New Ager who is now a committed believer in Christ told me after attending a seminar, which was being held in churches throughout the country, that he thought he was back in a New Age seminar. The seminar leaders were teaching a receptive audience of Christians about centering, visualization, sensing God's "active flow" within, having "SPIRIT-TO-SPIRIT encounters," "breaking through to the other side of silence," and many other occult and New Age principles and practices.

Many involved in Eastern, occult, and New Age beliefs erroneously use Psalm 46:10: "Be still, and know that I am God…"
to support such techniques as meditation or centering. However,
Scripture study will quickly reveal that "be still" literally means
to stop striving or struggling, tremble no more, because the Lord
is God. In other words, He wants us to completely rest in Him,
in His provision for us, and in His love for us. "Be still" does not
mean to put our minds in a neutral, passive mental state.

Don't Be Fooled by Hypnosis

"The word *hypnosis* is derived from the Greek word *hypnos*, meaning sleep… *Hypnotism* is a means of bringing on an artificial state
of sleep… more accurate[ly] a state of reduced consciousness."[5]

I went to research a hypnotist who was speaking on a uni-
versity campus. He was supposedly one of only four in the world
who could do instant hypnosis on people. There was an exciting
and energetic atmosphere in the auditorium that night. Many
young and undiscerning Christians could easily walk in there and
say, "Wow, this place is charged with the Spirit of God!"

As I looked around the auditorium, I recognized a Christian
in the audience. When the hypnotist called for volunteers, this
Christian went up, sat on the stage, and submitted his mind to a
man who had just demonstrated fortune-telling, divination, telepathy, and other occult practices (although he didn't call them that).

Where was this Christian's discernment? Where was his obedience to God's Word?

The hypnotist began to tell people whom he could not hypnotize to leave the stage, and the first person he told to leave was
this Christian. I believe God allowed that dismissal as his first

warning and was protecting him in spite of his carelessness and foolishness. But this person didn't heed that warning, for as soon as it was all over, he ran up to wait in line to see why this great hypnotist couldn't hypnotize him.

I believe the Lord sent me as his second warning. I went up and stood beside him and attempted to warn him of the potential danger of all this. I said, "What are you doing? This is occultism." He responded, "I don't worry about that stuff, I just read my Bible." I said, "Then you better *read* your Bible and see what it has to say about all this." He walked away a little irritated, but returned to me five minutes later when he overheard this hypnotist answering questions and discussing Tarot cards and other more obvious aspects of the occult.

Many were fooled because this hypnotist used scientific terminology, but his feats of mental and natural phenomena were a front for the occultism he was really promoting.

I received a personal interview with him after his program. He told me he considered himself a "good Christian" although he didn't believe in the Bible or that Jesus was the only way of salvation. I asked if he had ever considered the evidence for the uniqueness of Christ and the Bible, but he responded that he wasn't interested in that.

Although he wasn't open to considering that this phenomenon resulted from a demonic source, he told me he didn't really understand the source of his powers. "Maybe," he said, "it is from atomic energy or something like that," but he felt it was definitely beyond latent human powers.

He said he does not believe in occultism because that is supernaturalism, but he also told me palm reading, tea leaf reading, witchcraft, and so on can be beneficial to develop one's psychic abilities. From talking to him and reading the literature he gave me, I discovered he is a parapsychologist, psychic, and mind reader. He uses telepathy, does levitation, and practices meditation.

A Deadly Mixture

A brochure I received advertising a Christian Hypnosis Counseling Center sounded good on the surface. It promised to help you lose weight, quit smoking, release stress, and the like. If you continued to read, however, you would discover their true occult overtones. The brochure stated, "Universal energy takes you into a journey as you meet your spiritual guides."

This is the deadly mixture that is poisoning many Christians—terminology that sounds biblical or scientific causes many undiscerning believers to involve themselves in supposedly innocent techniques. They are subtly seduced away from pure devotion to Christ and His Word and are involved in imitation and counterfeit practices and experiences.

You may overcome your habit of smoking or gluttony through hypnosis, but do you know what often happens? A few days or weeks later some other problem manifests itself and another area of your life goes out of control. You keep succumbing to bad habits because you did not deal with the real problem, merely the symptom. God wants to get to the root cause, your need for discipline and self-control—which come only from obedience to His Word and the transforming work of the Holy Spirit.

Occult experts Wilson & Weldon write in their authoritative book, *Occult Shock:* "Our reasons for distrusting the use of hypnosis involve: (1) its possible similarity to the forbidden biblical practice of *charming;* (2) its historic origin to the occult in both the East (yoga) and West (Spiritist movement); (3) the fact that a wide variety of occult powers can be developed from hypnosis; (4) often past lives 'pop-up' during standard hypnotic regression, even when there is no expectation or searching for them; (5) cases of possession that have resulted; (6) the will must be surrendered to another person; (7) a similarity to mediumistic trance states…"[6]

Show Me in the Bible

Show me in Scripture where Jesus or Paul or anyone else used such techniques as hypnosis, visualization, imaging, or inner healing. You will not find them there. You will, however, find these techniques used in occultism.

Show me in God's Word where God's presence was attained or people had spiritual experiences through self-induced trances, visualization, imaging, or any other psychospiritual technique.

Visions or encounters with God in Scripture were not achieved through any techniques or self-induced methods, but through the divine intervention of a sovereign God (Genesis 15:1; 20:3; 31:24; 1 Kings 3:5; Daniel 10:1; Matthew 2:19; Acts 10:3; 16:9). That's why those who practice these techniques cannot give Scriptural validation for their involvement.

There are new discoveries and inventions such as electricity and cars that Jesus and Paul didn't use. But those are "physical" discoveries. I am talking about spiritual experiences. Jesus is God incarnate, the light of the world who came to show us the truth. Paul wrote much of the New Testament. If there were genuine techniques to bring us spiritual experiences and reality with our Creator, then Jesus Christ or Paul would surely have taught them to us. They didn't because these are counterfeit, occult techniques which would give us imitation and inferior spiritual experiences.

Many years ago, during my research of health and fitness, I was introduced to visualization techniques for healing. It seemed innocent enough and didn't appear to violate any biblical principles. Besides, it was recommended in a Christian book I was reading. As I closed my eyes and relaxed I began to create a mental image of being healthy. I visualized my body being healed and totally healthy. But I knew something was wrong and felt God's Spirit saying, "I do not want you doing this." I was obedient to God's Spirit and did not continue.

Shortly after that, I saw the film, *Gods of the New Age,* which revealed the occult and Eastern roots of this technique, and also confirmed what the Spirit was speaking to my heart. Because I had discernment and was determined to wholeheartedly follow the Lord, He protected me from something that could have jeopardized my walk with Him had I continued.

According to the *Omega Letter,* Michael Harner, a leading anthropologist (who endorses these New Age techniques), explained in his book, *The Way of the Shaman:*

Shaman is a word that anthropologists have adopted universally for what we used to call witch-doctors, medicine men, psychics, wizards, voodoo priests and so forth. It's witchcraft in other words... If you want to know what holistic medicine is, basically, it's simply a revival of witchcraft in the western world under new terms such as: visualization, aspects of psychotherapy, hypnotherapy, positive expressions for health and healing, positive confession, positive thinking. These all come out of witchcraft.

They've been practiced all around the world and you will find them in every culture on the face of this earth associated with shamanism. And now we are accepting them in the modern world under new terms...[7]

Always Keep Your Mind on Guard

Years ago I did extensive biblical research on spiritual warfare. I learned our minds are the spiritual battleground. No wonder God tells us to keep our minds on guard and protected. Putting our minds in a passive or neutral mental state is a doorway and steppingstone to the occult and opens us up to contact with spirit guides and familiar spirits (demonic entities).

James 4:7 says, "Submit yourselves therefore to God. Resist the devil, and he will flee from you." 2 Corinthians 10:5 states, "Casting down imaginations, and every high thing that exalteth itself against the knowledge of God, and bringing into captivity every thought to the obedience of Christ." Romans 12:2 says, "And be not conformed to this world: but be ye transformed by the renewing of your mind..."

Our minds need to be submitted to and controlled by the Lord Jesus Christ. In biblical meditation, our minds are filled with Scripture and are *actively* dwelling (like a cow chewing its cud) on God's Word.

The Mind is a Spiritual Battleground

The mind is a spiritual battleground where demonic activity, control, and manipulation occur. In 2 Corinthians 4:4, it states that, "the god of this world," referring to Satan, "hath blinded the minds of them which believe not, lest the light of the glorious gospel of Christ, who is the image of God, should shine unto them…"

So if Satan, according to Revelation 13:7, 8, is going to control the world, and if according to the apostle Paul in 2 Thessalonians 2:11, 12, God is going to send a strong delusion so that those who do not love the truth will believe the lie, how will this come to pass? *Through the mind.*

Consider all the mind-altering and hallucinogenic drugs, occult movies and cartoons, yoga, meditation, hypnosis, psycho-spiritual techniques, hyper-worship, ecstatic music, mind-expansion techniques, out-of-body experiences, and the many other methods and phenomena to put people into trance-like states or achieve altered states of consciousness. These are all ways to put your mind (the spiritual battleground) in a neutral, passive, non-resistant, and receptive mental state. In this state one can easily have thoughts implanted and be vulnerable to demonic manifestations and phenomena.

The world and even many Christians are being conditioned and programmed for a mass brainwashing and the greatest deception mankind has ever seen—the ultimate delusion prophesied in Scripture.

The purpose of the following illustration is twofold. First, to reveal and warn how many Christians are participating in spiritually dangerous occult techniques or "Christianized" versions. Second, it is to motivate you to take advantage of opportunities to share your faith in Christ during potential witness encounters.

Conscious Breathing Class

My wife Karen and I attended a two-week session at a health institute in San Diego. We knew the class on conscious breathing was going to be tainted with New Age techniques and beliefs, so Karen decided not to go. I looked at it as a research and witness opportunity. The instructor of this deep breathing class began by requesting everyone to close their eyes and hum a tone while punching the air to set the mood. Through "toning," practitioners learn to build up vibrations within the body as they hum and chant. The mystical connotations of sound, deep breathing, visualization, meditation, and energy flow were intended by the instructor to find application in holistic health treatment.

When I was the only one not participating, the instructor stopped the session and announced that everyone must participate. The toning and punching the air resumed but was abruptly stopped as the instructor asked if I was going to participate. With all eyes glaring at me, I told her that I would only do the breathing part. The instructor talked to me during a break, and I explained to her that it would be like her going to a fast food restaurant. She would have to be very selective in the choices she made so as not to violate her convictions. Besides, it would be a regression for her to consume what she believed to be inferior and potentially harmful food. I explained to her that in my spiritual walk, this is a regression.

The session resumed with about twenty-five people punching and dancing wildly while chanting tones, deep breathing, and saying positive affirmations. An audio-tape played for ninety minutes with music, toning, and such affirmations as: "You are beautiful," "You are whole," "You are divine," and "We are all children of God." While toning, deep breathing, and listening to the positive affirmations, participants were also told to visualize different colors as they visualized energy moving through the chakras. (In Hinduism, chakras are literally wheels or lotuses in the body which are emotional or spiritual centers, providing psychic information and energy. Chakras are the spiritual nerve center from the base of the spine to the crown of the head through which various energies, including the universal life force, are received, transformed, and distributed.)

During the session, the instructor twice invoked the gods of all who were there and also did an invocation for the masters of wisdom, inner guide, or whatever you believe the "mystery" to be. I felt like Joseph in Egypt and Daniel in Babylon. I was in an occult environment and inundated with their belief system. I responded in my mind to each affirmation with a biblical response. Now, I would not recommend any believer do what I did, but I prayed before attending this class and believed the Lord wanted me to see the influence many Christians are coming under and submitting to so I could both warn them and assure them of the superior power of God's Spirit and Word.

Immediately following the session several people came up to me and wanted to know why I would not participate. They listened intently for almost an hour as I shared my testimony of coming to know Jesus Christ and what He has done in my life. I then gave them copies of my *Spiritual Warfare* and *Who Is This Jesus?* books for further explanation. I was amazed at the number of people who, whilst participating in some blatant occult practices during the two weeks we were there, were professing Christians who should have had discernment and known better. Several attended evangelical and Pentecostal churches. A Jewish woman who also asked me why I would not participate listened intently as I shared how I searched for and found the Jewish Messiah and what her Hebrew Bible teaches concerning such occult involvement. She graciously received a copy of the *Who Is This Jesus?* book.

Near the end of the session one woman said, "I am a Christian and this just reaffirmed everything I believe." Another professing Christian woman enthusiastically participated in everything offered during the session. When it ended, she was smiling as if she had just seen Jesus. Another woman commented that her deceased grandmother was in the room with her during this.

I also attended a class on Advanced Alpha Techniques. It was taught by the same instructor who taught the conscious breathing class. Once again I did not participate in the techniques, but merely listened to the lectures.

Following this session the instructor had each of us share. Most told how stressed they were and their need to be in "alpha," a meditative, relaxed state. As my turn neared, I asked the Lord for wisdom concerning what to share. I told them I run a nonprofit organization that is often adventurous and chaotic, involving extreme stress at times, but that I have tremendous peace in the midst of it from my relationship with Jesus Christ.

After class, a woman approached me and said, "I need to talk to you." She told me she was a Christian and wanted to know how to sort this all out and what she could do to have the peace of the Lord. We had a long and fruitful conversation.

The next morning another woman approached me. She said she was Jewish and was greatly inspired by what I shared yesterday. She said she called her daughter after class to tell her what I said. Her daughter had just started a business in New York City and had several near disasters causing her to believe her new business was going to fail. She told me that what I shared in class greatly encouraged her daughter. I informed her I had been to Jerusalem many times and had a staff member who was a messianic believer. We had a good conversation and then parted because exercise class was beginning.

Many of the people attending these sessions were professing Christians indulging in all the New Age revelry. Others were seekers looking for new spiritual light and experiences or those hostile to Jesus Christ and offended by anything Christian.

As true believers in Jesus Christ living in a growing pagan society, we must be light in the midst of darkness and salt that has not become tasteless without compromising our biblical convictions. Having this "balance" may be a challenge in this day and age, but it is tremendously crucial.

Venice Beach Experiences

Venice Beach in Southern California was known as Muscle Beach in the 1960s. It was the place all my weight lifting buddies and I dreamed of going when we were teens. A few years ago, while ministering in California, I had the opportunity to visit Venice Beach with two of my nephews who lived in Southern California.

As the Apostle Paul observed and examined the idols in Athens before reasoning in the marketplace and speaking to the philosophers in the Areopagus, I evaluated the environment and mindset at Venice Beach before interacting with the people and passing out some of my books and pamphlets.

One area of the beach had fitness equipment and gymnastic apparatuses so I began there. In an attempt to get myself acclimated before interacting with the people—and maybe to fulfill a teenage dream—I climbed to the top of a high rope, did a few feats on the gymnastic rings and parallel bars, and punched the speed bag. Now I was ready to interact with the people.

Lined along the beach was a seemingly endless array of booths displaying every imaginable philosophy from hate Christ, the Bible stinks and Jesus is a fake, to, give your kids pot and pot for babies, to, animal rights and gay activists, to, psychics, fortune-tellers, and Tarot card readers.

At one of the booths an elderly Caucasian woman and her much younger African American husband were dressed in bathrobes. After engaging them in conversation for several minutes to discover the philosophy they were propogating I gave the woman a copy of my book, *Who Is This Jesus*. She was warmly excited and asked if she could really keep it—as virtually everything there is for sale. When I said, "Sure," she promised she would read it.

After talking to people at several more booths I felt drawn to a booth displaying a large sign advertising a master Tarot card reader. I love to engage leading occultists and New Agers in conversation concerning Jesus Christ and the Bible. So, in hope of gaining an opportunity to share with this master of divination and fortune-telling, I asked him how he came to his journey of spiritual revelation.

Fascinated by my question he asked me to sit with him at his booth as he shared the story of his spiritual journey and I interjected questions and comments. We talked for almost an hour as he actually chased away potential customers by saying, "Can't you see that I am in a fascinating conversation?"

He was an accountant and was almost finished writing a book revealing the secret that he said will bring peace to our nation and world within fifty years. He stated that God speaks to him directly and the Bible is inaccurate and Jesus could not be the only way because we are all divine. According to him, everyone needed to have a marriage of their inner female and inner male self to attain enlightenment and become one.

Finally he asked me to tell him my spiritual journey. This was the opportunity for which I waited. Had I not listened to him, he would have never listened to me.

The sharing of my testimony and our interaction resulted in an incredible opportunity to present Jesus' unique claims, prophecies concerning His Second Coming, and one's eternal destiny. I was able to share the whole plan of salvation with a man who would have otherwise rejected it outright. My prayer is that the Holy Spirit deals with this man in such a way that he comes to know the true Prince of Peace and has real answers to life and eternity.

The philosophies being expounded at many of the booths might seem bizarre to some but they are being accepted by multitudes of youth and adults across our nation and world. All this would be laughable if the reality was not so diabolically dangerous and deadly. Millions of people—even many who were raised in church—have been influenced by similar philosophies. Many more of our young people are being stripped of their biblical faith while attending colleges and universities. And numerous formerly professing Christians have renounced faith in the biblical Jesus for foolish and vain philosophies.

Do you realize that when I research or have encounters with those adhering to New Age and occult beliefs, my mind is in an analytical mode? I am critiquing, evaluating, and sifting everything through God's Word. I have spent time in prayer and fasting to have discernment from His Spirit. But when youth and adults sit there being entertained or participate in activities with an attitude of receptivity they are violating God's clear scriptural warning concerning what should fill our minds. A gradual desensitization, indoctrination, and transition often occurs—eventually altering one's worldview.

If you think New Age philosophies and practices are innocent then consider an ad in a New Age magazine selling T-shirts with the following on it, "Your God requires blood sacrifice, subjugation of women, annihilation of cities, slaughter of multitudes, unquestioned obedience, murder of His own son, destruction by flood, and as a grand finale, He plans to destroy the world by fire! And you ask me why I'm a Pagan?"

Out of context these accusations seem to make sense and could cause one to question God and reject the Bible but when you evaluate these comments in the context of Scripture and history, they can easily be refuted. But young people who do not know God's Word or have a strong relationship with the Lord can be easily swayed with such hostile philosophies that seek to undermine biblical faith and values. Pastors and Christian leaders who ignorantly or supposedly innocently open their churches to any kind of New Age or occult beliefs and practices are unleashing great spiritual harm.

Believers who want to stand in these days of increasing deception need discernment —which comes by studying Scripture and knowing the voice of His Spirit as a result of spending time with the Lord in prayer and fasting. Courage and love are also needed if one is to gain opportunities to share Christ with those who may be hostile to the Gospel or have distorted perspectives of biblical Christianity.

Like the Tarot card reader at Venice Beach, we must look at each person as someone for whom Jesus Christ died. Although we may disagree with them or even hate the philosophy or lifestyle they represent, we must display respect. Also, we must not be intimidated or fearful but go on their turf and to their meetings to share the genuine love, truth, and power of Jesus Christ.

Called to Be a Shaman

A teenager who had once been a seemingly committed believer was taken by his parents to a "signs and wonders" church frequently visited by the "prophets" and where unbiblical phenomena disguised as the Holy Spirit frequently occurred. He and his parents eventually had enough of the bizarre behavior and left for a safer church. But like many young people and adults exposed to a distorted and often perverted form of Christianity, he rejected genuine biblical Christianity along with the imitation and counterfeit he experienced at the previous church.

About a year later I met him while walking in the park. I asked him how he was doing with the Lord. He related that God had been speaking to him every day. He said, "He has called me to be a shaman. I am just waiting for Him to send me a teacher." His eyes widened in surprise as I related how I had led a shaman to Christ. "This shaman," I said, "left his darkness and came to the light. So why is the Lord leading you to leave the light and go back to the darkness?" He replied, "I don't believe shamanism is 'darkness.' I believe we can learn truth about God and Jesus through all religions." Before we parted I encouraged him to read the Gospel of John and 1 John.

Our Young People Are Being Seduced

I have warned how our young people are being seduced by the occultism they are exposed to through the media, school, and even in some churches. There is a price to pay by parents who allow their children to watch movies and television shows, listen to music, play video games, and participate in activities with occult overtones, or attend churches and conferences where unscriptural teaching and phenomena are occurring.

It may initially seem harmless, but in the end it could prove fatal. The world is filled with Christians who have been sabotaged and shipwrecked in their faith because of false teachings and unbiblical techniques. One day these parents will be heartbroken as they face the tragic consequences of defiant children who reject the Jesus of the Bible and clear biblical teachings.

Yoga and Martial Arts in the Church

While some pastors are refusing to compromise biblical Christianity, others are welcoming yoga and seemingly innocent martial art classes into their churches, allowing an unholy mix of New Age philosophies and practices. Who will the Lord commend—the pastor who tries to grow a church by blending Christianity with New Age, occult, and Eastern mysticism, or the pastor who protects his flock from seductive and dangerous teachings and practices?

I believe the words Jesus spoke to the church in Pergamum (a church that did not deny His name but allowed an unholy mix of false teachings and unbiblical practices) are His words of rebuke to many pastors and churches today—"But I have a few things against thee, because thou hast there them that hold the doctrine of Balaam, who taught Balac to cast a stumblingblock before the children of Israel, to eat things sacrificed unto idols, and to commit fornication. So hast thou also them that hold the doctrine of the Nicolaitans, which thing I hate. Repent; or else I will come unto thee quickly, and will fight against them with the sword of my mouth" (Revelation 2:14–16).

Hundreds of young people and adults have shared with me the eventual spiritual oppression and confusion they encountered through martial arts and yoga practices. Many who wanted to serve the Lord wholeheartedly went through years of anguish in unraveling the techniques and philosophies they were taught that enveloped their minds and hearts. For more information on the potential spiritual dangers of the martial arts, request my booklets *Why I Quit Karate* and *Self-Defense from a Biblical Perspective*.

New Age and Immoral Encounters at a Health Center

A couple of years ago, my wife and I attended a health clinic in Southern California for one week. It focused on physical, mental, and spiritual health. Most was from a New Age perspective, so our involvement was limited to exercise, wheat grass juice, and organic salads.

People there were involved in everything from various styles of the martial arts, yoga, meditation, chanting, toning, visualization, and recognizing the god within, to "the Golden serpent moving with energy up their spines and to their heads."

All this seemed like love and spirituality on the surface—but underneath was rejection of the Creator, pride and egotism, and in many cases, subtle or blatant immorality and idolatry.

Interestingly, what was visibly manifest were the very two things that repeatedly took down Israel—idolatry/false gods and sexual immorality. No wonder the admonition of Acts 15:29 to the early church included abstaining from food sacrificed to idols and sexual immorality. God knows our human weakness and where the enemy focuses his deceptive attacks.

Initially, we thought the Lord led us there to be a witness for Him as we had during our previous visits. But at the end of our stay this time we realized the Lord sent us there for another reason—to expose this new spirituality sweeping our country and world. We both also determined in our hearts that no matter what the health benefits were, we would not return.

The people—many who had a Christian background— rejected Jesus without ever knowing Him. Others had been steeped in mysticism and occultism their whole lives.

A seventy-six-year-old business man told me he rejected Christianity (Catholicism) in his thirties because he felt closer to God on LSD than doing "Hail Mary's." He spent the rest of his life in every New Age and Eastern mystical experience imaginable. When I asked him his concept of eternal life, he said he believed God is spirit and will be a he or a she, or personal or impersonal—he wasn't sure. He believes when he dies it will be darkness, but his spirit will live on and he will be able to escape the darkness through meditation. He actually encouraged me to reject Christianity and embrace his belief system—a chaotic mess of confusion and hopelessness.

There was absolutely nothing impressive in this man or anyone else there that I desired in the least. It only showed me how amazing and superior the Gospel of Jesus Christ is. Karen's and my daily Bible studies that week were in the books of Philippians and Colossians, which reveal Christ's surpassing greatness.

Our spirits were grieved. Many times I fell on my knees and prayed with Karen in our room, "O Lord, how can we reach these people?" They would accept and tolerate anything and everything—except biblical Christianity.

During the testimony time and talent show some of them praised the gods who provided wheat grass and others praised the gods within. They used vulgar language, engaged in opposite and same sex kissing on the lips, and flaunted licentious behavior.

Many people I knew from my youth rejected Christ because they wanted to continue in their immoral lifestyles. However, these people embraced a spirituality that allowed them to feel connected to *God* while continuing any lifestyle and pursuit they desired. But their source of spirituality was obvious from their conversations and behavior.

As we prayed for these people, and wondered why we could not reach even one as we had during two previous stays at this clinic, the Lord spoke to my heart that they had become like the people in Sodom and Gomorrah during Lot's time—none repented.

It was as though they were under a strong seductive influence, like the people at the golden calf (Exodus 32), or the Israelites at Shittim, when the men sinned with the Moabite women and offered sacrifices to their gods (Numbers 25).

These people had seared consciences and reprobate minds. It was obvious from what they were willing to accept—virtually anything—and what they openly rejected—the light of the glorious gospel of Christ. Because they did not love the truth, a strong delusion had overtaken them.

Many people are rapidly moving in this same direction of false spirituality and immorality. Time is short and this nation and world are rapidly changing. We must reach as many people as possible with the true gospel while we still have opportunity.

It is imperative we stand strong in our faith in Christ and keep our lives and churches pure and untainted by an unholy mix. We must provide our children and young people clear and accurate biblical instruction so they can discern what is false.

Ad in a New Age Magazine

Millan, author, lecturer, and nutritionist in San Diego deals with many people involved in New Age and Eastern mystical practices. She writes:

Dear Bill,

I have placed the following ad in a New Age, metaphysical magazine to lead those who are struggling with demonic torment or attack to the saving knowledge of Jesus and the power of His Holy Spirit. The ad stated: "Being Bothered, Attacked, Disturbed or Tormented by Spirits? Call for confidential help and freedom..."

Millan continues:

My twenty-seven years in the alternative health field has led me to the conclusion that many people who meditate and practice yoga, open themselves up to tormenting spirits by inviting "spirit guides" into their lives. At first these spirits seem helpful and necessary for one to experience a new level of spirituality. As they continue to encounter and enhance these spirits, they discover another side as these spirits become dangerous, ugly, and threatening.

That individual then is perplexed and sometimes becomes suicidal. Only God's Holy Spirit and His power can bring victory in defeating these spirits that play havoc on one's life.

Our precious Lord has already enabled me to lead nineteen individuals to the saving knowledge of Him through this ad, and with continued prayer, hopefully many more who need Jesus Christ and His precious love.

I give them or mail them a Bible, an outline of instructions in their new life, and oftentimes your book Spiritual Warfare *and* Victory in Christ.

God bless you and keep you for His own.

Chapter Four

IS POSITIVE CONFESSION
THE SECRET TO RECEIVING
GOD'S BLESSING?

I believe in having a positive attitude. I see too many negative, pessimistic, complaining, whining, and defeated Christians who are controlled by worry, fear, jealousy, bitterness, revenge, and hopelessness. The internal stress of these negative and destructive emotions can make you sick and turn people off to the Gospel. Love, joy, peace, and hope are attitudes conducive to good health and to being a good witness.

During the early years of my ministry, I was asked to visit a young man who had been admitted to the hospital with stomach pains. When I arrived he was in the intensive care unit with pancreatitis. His condition went from bad to worse and it appeared there was little hope for him to survive.

Before he was transferred to a hospital in Pittsburgh, I was able to see him several times. Although he was unable to respond, and although the nurses said he was unable to hear me, I knew his mind could comprehend what I was saying. So I shared words of encouragement and quoted Scriptures such as Philippians 4:13, "I can do all things through Christ which strengtheneth me," in an attempt to give him hope and courage. I let him know that we would stand with him and continue to pray until he came through this crisis. I also used Scripture to convince him how important his mental attitude was at this time, and that he must not give up!

In Pittsburgh, he had a dramatic recovery. When he finally came home, he said, "The only thing I remember about the first hospital was a young man who repeatedly entered my room. He would quote Scripture and reassure me that I could make it!"

When he finally found out who I was, he informed me that my encouraging him and giving him hope was one of the main things that helped him recover. His wife thanked me for saving her husband's life.

Positive?... Yes—Presumptuous?... No!

I am probably one of the most positive, optimistic people you will ever meet. I have attempted to build my life and ministry on such biblical principles as determination, faith, courage, obedience, discipline, commitment, love, joy, and peace. These are very positive. I believe in having "positive" and unwavering faith as I take on challenges, face giants, attempt to do exploits for the Lord, and believe God to do the impossible through my life and ministry.

While I do believe in these biblical principles, I do not believe in telling God what I want with a "give me" mentality. I do not believe in usurping God's Lordship and sovereignty by trying to force, coerce, or manipulate Him to respond by using the right formula or technique.

While the positive confession concept as a new Christian encouraged me to walk in faith and confidence and victory, I also began to notice a growing distortion of its truth. It got out of biblical balance. When we begin confessing our will and desires into existence or when we teach that whatever we want, we just confess it and believe it and we have it—that is more like the occultism I abandoned and less and less like the Scripture I was studying.

I believe there is a very subtle line between standing in faith while confessing His will, and being in rebellion by attempting to control God through self-centered, self-motivated confession. We are not dealing with an impersonal energy force—but the awesome, personal, infinite God of the Bible who is sovereign Lord over the universe.

Attempting to create or alter reality contrary to His will through the "power of faith" and "positive confession" is really a form of "Christianized sorcery."

"Divine Health" in a Fallen World?

There are people who claim they walk in divine health. This is easy to do when one is young and healthy but more difficult as one ages. Just give me five minutes with anyone who believes or teaches this and I can easily show how utterly absurd and foolish it is by pointing out "symptoms of decay" in their own bodies. All of us manifest evidence of less-than-ideal health.

I am in better physical shape and live a healthier life than most Christians I have met, yet I cannot be deluded to think I have achieved divine health. I realize I am in a fallen world with a slowly deteriorating body. Although I have excellent health, the constant "giving of my body" for the sake of the Gospel takes its toll. Paul states in 2 Corinthians 4:16, "For which cause we faint not; but though our outward man perish, yet the inward man is renewed day by day." I am waiting for this body to be transformed into a perfect resurrected body at the Lord's return (Romans 8:18–25; 1 Corinthians 15:35–57; Philippians 3:20, 21).

Until my Lord returns I will take care of my body, the temple of the Holy Spirit, that I might better serve Him. Living by the biblical principles of health and nutrition have proved far superior to any other lifestyle available.

"Selfianity"

In many circles Christianity has been replaced by what I call "Selfianity." "Selfianity" is people serving God for what they can get from Him. As long as He is blessing them they honor Him; when the prosperity terminates, so does their commitment. People who adhere to "Selfianity" want to be their own gods, declare their own futures, decree their own destinies, and fulfill their own dreams and desires.

"Selfianity" is a subtle twisting of Scripture—actually a total reversal of what God's Word teaches in context. Behind the facade of biblical terminology and supposed exaltation of Christ, lurks a philosophy of self-centeredness, rebellion against the God of the Bible, and sorcery.

A sorcerer seeks to use the proper spells, incantations, formulas, and rituals to control people and circumstances, to obtain their intended purpose. Many professing believers in Jesus seek to manipulate God in similar fashion through "proper" confession.

A woman who was having problems with her car was praying for someone to come and give her a ride. When I walked in, she was very discouraged; so, as I gave her a ride, I began to share some of the highlights concerning how God provided our "miracle van" when it was totally impossible.

She became very encouraged and excited and said, "Are you into prosperity?" I responded, "I am into the Lord! All that matters to me is Jesus Christ. I do not serve Him for what He gives me. I serve Him because of who He is." I have learned like Paul, "to be content. I know both how to be abased, and I know how to abound: every where and in all things I am instructed both to be full and to be hungry, both to abound and to suffer need. I can do all things through Christ which strengtheneth me" (Philippians 4:11–13).

Then she asked, "Well, did you confess this van into being?" I responded, "No, I got on my knees, prayed, fasted, and asked, 'Father, what is Your will? You know the future. You know which vehicle we need for our ministry. You know all things. Please show us Your will, and fulfill and perform Your will in this situation.' So He showed us His will, and it was to get this van. And then for months as the van sat unsold in the car dealer's lot, we trusted God to provide the necessary funds. He faithfully intervened in some incredible ways to provide this 'miracle van.'"

Are you confessing and asserting your will or praying for God's will and submitting to the leading of His Spirit? Are you attempting to force God to give you what you want now or trusting Him to fulfill His purpose and do what is ultimately best?

Don't be deceived into wasting your life on "Selfianity" and seeking to be your own god. Why settle for vain philosophies and imitation techniques which are far inferior to what the Holy Spirit and obedience to God's Word can accomplish in your life?

Satan Exalted Himself...
Christ Humbly Obeyed

Who made some of the most positive confessions in the Bible? Satan. He spoke such positive statements as: "Ye shall not surely die: For God doth know that in the day ye eat thereof, then your eyes shall be opened, and ye shall be as gods, knowing good and evil" (Genesis 3:4, 5).

Another positive confession is found in Isaiah 14. It says concerning the "king of Babylon," "For thou hast said in thine heart, I will ascend into heaven, I will exalt my throne above the stars of God: I will sit also upon the mount of the congregation, in the sides of the north: I will ascend above the heights of the clouds; I will be like the most High" (Isaiah 14:13, 14).

But God said: "Yet thou shalt be brought down to hell, to the sides of the pit" (Isaiah 14:15).

The problem with this type of positive confession is that it is *positively wrong*. In contrast, Philippians 2:5–8 states, regarding Christ, "Let this mind be in you, which was also in Christ Jesus: Who, being in the form of God, thought it not robbery to be equal with God: But made himself of no reputation, and took upon him the form of a servant, and was made in the likeness of men: And being found in fashion as a man, he humbled himself, and became obedient unto death, even the death of the cross."

As a result of this, the outcome for Jesus is the exact opposite of what happened to Satan. Philippians 2:9–11 states, "Wherefore God also hath highly exalted him, and given him a name which is above every name: That at the name of Jesus every knee should bow, of things in heaven, and things in earth, and things under the earth; And that every tongue should confess that Jesus Christ is Lord, to the glory of God the Father."

Stand in God's Will

When I gave my life to Jesus Christ, I dethroned self. I am not about to return to that former lifestyle. I do not want to play God, exert my godhood, decree my will, or replace His Lordship with my own.

Many Christians fall away after they go through difficult times or when God doesn't give them what they want. They often fall because they have been taught an unscriptural Christianity and have not made Christ Lord of their lives.

My responsibility is to do what Jesus did—humble myself, be obedient to the Father's will, and exalt and glorify Him. I frequently get on my knees in prayer and fasting to seek His will and know His Word and Spirit. Then I stand in His strength, proclaim His will, and walk in obedience until He fulfills it.

When we operate from this Scriptural foundation, we are assured of God's provision, empowering, and the fulfillment of His promises.

When our ministry was still very young, my wife and I and our two children lived in an apartment. As the ministry continued to grow, we looked for a house to move into so we could have our offices in the basement. Instead of opening just one door so we could conveniently walk through it, God opened two doors simultaneously so we would have to make a decision.

The one house was very large and ideal for my objectives. The other house was much smaller and not as adequate. And everyone said, "Bill, you are a child of the King. You tell God what you want and He will give it to you." I replied, "There is something wrong with that. I am not God. I cannot foresee the future. In my limited foresight I cannot determine which will ultimately be the best decision. I do not know the end result; I do not know what God's total plan is. I walk by faith, not by sight."

Then I said, "What I am going to do is this: instead of me telling God what to do, I am going to get on my knees. I am going to pray and fast and find out what His will is, and then I will be obedient to how He leads. I will stand and confess His will, not mine."

God spoke to my heart to move into the smaller house. In obedience, I did. For months I wondered why. I said, "You know I trust You Lord, but that other house was so much nicer and much more adequate." And He spoke to my heart, "Trust Me!"

A few months later, we had 3.7 acres of prime land donated to us. The land was located behind the house we were renting and was appraised at $80,000 back in 1981. Shortly thereafter, the Lord strongly led us to step out in faith and build a ministry center on this property. The Lord intervened in a mighty way, enabling us to overcome many *giants* and complete a half-million-dollar project without a penny of interest being paid. If I had moved into the larger, more adequate house, I would have missed the tremendous blessing and victory God gave to us for obeying His will and not seeking our own.

Do not tell God what you want Him to do. Do not try to

force God to do your will. Get on your knees and pray and fast and seek His will. Then stand in faith until He fulfills what He has led you to do.

My prayer for guidance is often something like: "Lord, give me sensitivity and discernment from your Word and Spirit, unwavering faith to believe You, and obedience to do what You lead me to do." And then I trust Him who "always causeth us to triumph in Christ, and maketh manifest the savour of his knowledge by us in every place" (2 Corinthians 2:14).

There have been countless miracles in my life and ministry. But before the Lord intervened in what He led me to step out in faith and do I repeatedly heard people say: "That is impossible! You can't do it!" And they were right—by myself I couldn't. But an all-powerful God intervened and made the impossible *possible*. He did so because I was seeking His will, not my own. I was walking in obedience to His Word and the leading of His Spirit. I was seeking to glorify Him, not myself.

First Seek the Lord—His Blessing Will Follow

Instead of determining what I want God's will to be, then hoping He blesses my decision, I seek the Lord with all my heart through prayer, fasting, and reading Scripture. Until He gives clear direction, I walk by faith using wisdom as I live by biblical principles.

I have discovered a pattern in Scripture and have witnessed it in my life and ministry repeatedly. Once the Lord leads me to do something and I step out in faith and obedience, more often than not, just about everything imaginable goes wrong. It seems impossible to be fulfilled and defeat seems apparent. Then the

Lord intervenes in His time and way and is faithful to bring ultimate victory. This way He alone gets the glory.

The many blessings and miracles God has bestowed in my life, family, and ministry are not a reality because of "proper confession" or using the "right technique" but because of faith in Him and obedience to His Word. I have not sought these things, but have sought Him—to know and obey His will, and to make Him Lord over every aspect of my life. As a result, He has greatly honored and blessed me in ways too numerous to mention.

But I don't serve Him for prosperity. My main motivation is not merely to receive His blessing. For if He removes His hand of blessing (as He has occasionally done) I still serve and honor Him.

The Lord has also blessed me financially, but I have chosen to give most of it away and live a moderate lifestyle. I could easily be justified in having a salary two or three times more than I do, but I have chosen to use that money to spread the Gospel throughout the world.

Some people spend so much of their time and energy trying to get God to give them wealth and prosperity. But honoring Him has proven to be the wisest path. Besides, Scripture repeatedly indicates that spiritual riches are far more important than material wealth. Jesus said, "Lay not up for yourselves treasures upon earth, where moth and rust doth corrupt, and where thieves break through and steal: But lay up for yourselves treasures in heaven…" (Matthew 6:19–20).

In Ephesians 2:6, 7, Paul speaks of the "exceeding riches" of God's grace which we find in the "heavenly places." In Colossians 3:1–2, he admonishes us to set our "affection on things above, not on things on the earth." We are commanded in 1 Timothy to "be rich in good works," which will lay up treasure for us in the coming age (6:18, 19).

The heroes of the faith gave up the pleasures of this world to focus on eternal riches and blessings. For example, see Hebrews 11:8–10 concerning Abraham.

Keep Scripture in Context

You cannot take Scriptural passages out of context and expect to build sound theology. Study Scripture in context to rightly divide the word of truth (2 Timothy 2:15) so as to obtain a clearer and more "balanced" understanding. This will safeguard you from the extreme perspectives and distortions many come to from taking verses out of context or approaching the Bible with preconceived ideas.

Also realize, Scripture interprets Scripture. Part of a truth might be found in the book of John and an additional insight in James or Hebrews. Scripture must be treated as a whole.

John 14:14 states, "If ye shall ask any thing in my name, I will do it." Many Christians quote this verse out of context and make the erroneous conclusion that whatever they ask of God, He is obligated to do. But they ignore the next verse which gives the biblical balance, "If ye love me, keep my commandments" (John 14:15). And if you truly love Him and are obeying His Word then whatever you ask for would be consistent with His will.

Be careful not to focus only on God's promises and blessings and forget His inherent requirements and responsibilities. People who use verses out of context or resort to gimmicks and techniques such as reciting special prayers and confessions of faith in an attempt to achieve their own desires and goals are wasting their time. Like the grass and flowers of the field, they and their selfish desires will soon fade away.

I believe the main Scriptural criteria for receiving and maintaining God's blessings in both this life and eternity are obedience and faithfulness to Him. Deuteronomy 30:8 reads, "And thou shalt return and obey the voice of the LORD, and do all his commandments which I command thee this day." As a result, Deuteronomy 30:9 promises, "And the LORD thy God will make thee plenteous in every work of thine hand, in the fruit of thy body, and in the fruit of thy cattle, and in the fruit of thy land, for good…"

Deuteronomy chapters 28–30 reveal that obedience results in receiving God's blessing, while those who are disobedient will be cursed by God (no matter what they confess).

Don't be fooled. Material wealth is not necessarily the evidence of God's blessing. Some of the most righteous people throughout the pages of Scripture and history suffered great persecution and lived in less than ideal conditions. Their wealth was not in physical objects, but in their rich relationship with the Lord.

Leviticus chapter 26 is also about being blessed because of obedience and being cursed because of disobedience. In fact, the only "confession" we see in this chapter dealing with God's blessings/curses is in verse 40, and it is in regard to "confessing their iniquity."

Principles on Prayer

As I sought the Lord concerning a prayer request, He impressed on my heart several Scriptural truths and principles that should all be working simultaneously. The following are a few highlights:

1) Right Motives:

James 4:3: "Ye ask, and receive not, because ye ask amiss, that ye may consume it upon your lusts."

2) According to His Will:

1 John 5:14: "And this is the confidence that we have in him, that, if we ask any thing according to his will, he heareth us."

3) Persistence:

Luke 11:5–10:

> And he said unto them, Which of you shall have a friend, and shall go unto him at midnight, and say unto him, Friend, lend me three loaves; For a friend of mine in his journey is come to me, and I have nothing to set before him? And he from within shall answer and say, Trouble me not: the door is now shut, and my children are with me in bed; I cannot rise and give thee. I say unto you, Though he will not rise and give him, because he is his friend, yet because of his importunity he will rise and give him as many as he needeth. And I say unto you, Ask, and it shall be given you; seek, and ye shall find; knock, and it shall be opened unto you. For every one that asketh receiveth; and he that seeketh findeth; and to him that knocketh it shall be opened.

4) Do Not Doubt:

James 1:6, 7: "But let him ask in faith, nothing wavering. For he that wavereth is like a wave of the sea driven with the wind and tossed. For let not that man think that he shall receive any thing of the Lord."

Hebrews 11:1, 6: "Now faith is the substance of things hoped for, the evidence of things not seen. But without faith it is impossible to please him: for he that cometh to God must believe that he is, and that he is a rewarder of them that diligently seek him."

5) Mountain-Moving Faith:

Mark 9:23: "Jesus said unto him, If thou canst believe, all things are possible to him that believeth."

Mark 11:23: "For verily I say unto you, That whosoever shall say unto this mountain, Be thou removed, and be thou cast into the sea; and shall not doubt in his heart, but shall believe that those things which he saith shall come to pass; he shall have whatsoever he saith."

6) Do Not Be Anxious—Be Thankful:

Philippians 4:6, 7: "Be careful for nothing; but in every thing by prayer and supplication with thanksgiving let your requests be made known unto God. And the peace of God, which passeth all understanding, shall keep your hearts and minds through Christ Jesus."

Colossians 4:2: "Continue in prayer, and watch in the same with thanksgiving."

7) Obedience:

John 14:14, 15: "If ye shall ask any thing in my name, I will do it. If ye love me, keep my commandments."

John 15:7: "If ye abide in me, and my words abide in you, ye shall ask what ye will, and it shall be done unto you."

1 John 3:21–24: "Beloved, if our heart condemn us not, then have we confidence toward God. And whatsoever we ask, we receive of him, because we keep his commandments, and do

those things that are pleasing in his sight. And this is his commandment, That we should believe on the name of his Son Jesus Christ, and love one another, as he gave us commandment. And he that keepeth his commandments dwelleth in him, and he in him. And hereby we know that he abideth in us, by the Spirit which he hath given us."

8) Clean Heart Before God:
2 Chronicles 6:36–39:

> If they sin against thee, (for there is no man which sinneth not,) and thou be angry with them, and deliver them over before their enemies, and they carry them away captives unto a land far off or near; Yet if they bethink themselves in the land whither they are carried captive, and turn and pray unto thee in the land of their captivity, saying, We have sinned, we have done amiss, and have dealt wickedly; If they return to thee with all their heart and with all their soul in the land of their captivity, whither they have carried them captives, and pray toward their land, which thou gavest unto their fathers, and toward the city which thou hast chosen, and toward the house which I have built for thy name: Then hear thou from the heavens, even from thy dwelling place, their prayer and their supplications, and maintain their cause, and forgive thy people which have sinned against thee.

2 Chronicles 7:14: "If my people, which are called by my name, shall humble themselves, and pray, and seek my face, and turn from their wicked ways; then will I hear from heaven, and will forgive their sin, and will heal their land."

Psalm 66:18: "If I regard iniquity in my heart, the Lord will not hear me."

Isaiah 1:15–17: "And when ye spread forth your hands, I will hide mine eyes from you: yea, when ye make many prayers, I will not hear: your hands are full of blood. Wash you, make you clean; put away the evil of your doings from before mine eyes; cease to do evil; Learn to do well; seek judgment, relieve the oppressed, judge the fatherless, plead for the widow."

James 5:16–18: "Confess your faults one to another, and pray one for another, that ye may be healed. The effectual fervent prayer of a righteous man availeth much. Elias was a man subject to like passions as we are, and he prayed earnestly that it might not rain: and it rained not on the earth by the space of three years and six months. And he prayed again, and the heaven gave rain, and the earth brought forth her fruit."

9) Delight Yourself in the Lord:
Psalm 37:4: "Delight thyself also in the LORD: and he shall give thee the desires of thine heart."

Matthew 6:33: "But seek ye first the kingdom of God, and his righteousness; and all these things shall be added unto you."

The Lord has taught me that I cannot manipulate Him to give me what I want. But if I delight myself in Him, seek His will, and walk in obedience to it, He will grant the desires of my heart (because they will be His desires as well) and abundantly bless beyond what I could ever ask or think—beyond my greatest expectations.

Chapter Five

IS MUCH OF TODAY'S "PROPHESYING" IN REALITY "CHRISTIANIZED FORTUNE-TELLING"?

There are two *extreme* positions concerning prophecy: 1) To "despise" prophetic utterance and thereby "quench" the Spirit; and 2) To encourage or tolerate a form of prophecy that is unscriptural.

I believe that prophecy is for today. I believe the New Testament indicates that the gift of prophecy should be in operation in the Church (1 Corinthians 12; 1 Corinthians 14; Ephesians 4:11; 1 Thessalonians 5:20, 21; 1 Timothy 4:14). In 1 Corinthians 14:39, Paul encourages believers to "desire earnestly to prophesy..." But I do not believe in endorsing the tremendous misuse and abuse of this gift today. I will not tolerate those who speak from their own inspiration nor the demonic counterfeits, which are being enthusiastically received in many Christian circles.

The *Expository Dictionary of Bible Words* states: "The basic word for 'prophet' in the OT is *nabi*, which means 'spokesman' or 'speaker.' Essentially a prophet is a person authorized to speak for another, as Moses (Exodus 7:1–2; Numbers 12:1–8) and the OT prophets were authorized to speak for God... The Greek word *prophetes* (prophet) is the only word the NT uses to translate the Hebrew *nabi*. Related NT words are *propheteuo* ('to prophesy'), *prophetis* ('prophetess'), and *propheteia* ('prophetic saying, gift, or activity')."[8]

Two Types of False Prophets

There are two main types of false prophets in the Bible. First, there are those who speak and prophesy in the name of other gods such as Baal (Jeremiah 2:8; 23:13; 32:32–35). This type of false prophet is very easy to distinguish, but it gets more difficult and confusing when we deal with the second type of false prophets.

There are false prophets who claim to prophesy in the name of the Lord; yet, they are proclaiming the word that the Lord has not told them to proclaim. A few examples follow:

Jeremiah 14:14: "Then the LORD said unto me, The prophets prophesy lies in my name: I sent them not, neither have I commanded them, neither spake unto them: they prophesy unto you a false vision and divination, and a thing of nought, and the deceit of their heart."

Jeremiah 23:16, 21, 22, 30–32:

Thus saith the LORD of hosts, Hearken not unto the words of the prophets that prophesy unto you: they make you vain: they speak a vision of their own heart, and not out of the mouth of the LORD... I have not sent these prophets, yet they ran: I have not spoken to them, yet they prophesied. But if they had stood in my counsel, and had caused my people to hear my words, then they should have turned them from their evil way, and from the evil of their doings. Therefore, behold, I am against the prophets, saith the LORD, that steal my words every one from his neighbour... Behold, I am against the prophets, saith the LORD, that use their tongues, and say, He saith. Behold, I am against them that prophesy false dreams, saith the LORD, and do tell them, and cause my people to err by their lies, and by their lightness; yet I sent them not, nor commanded them: therefore they shall not profit this people at all, saith the LORD.

Ezekiel 13:2, 3, 6, 8: "Son of man, prophesy against the prophets of Israel that prophesy, and say thou unto them that prophesy out of their own hearts, Hear ye the word of the LORD; Thus saith the Lord GOD; Woe unto the foolish prophets, that follow their own spirit, and have seen nothing!... They have seen vanity and lying divination, saying, The LORD saith: and the LORD hath not sent them: and they have made others to hope that they would confirm the word. Therefore thus saith the Lord GOD; Because ye have spoken vanity, and seen lies, therefore, behold, I am against you, saith the Lord GOD."

Matthew 7:22, 23: "Many will say to me in that day, Lord, Lord, have we not prophesied in thy name? and in thy name have cast out devils? and in thy name done many wonderful works? And then will I profess unto them, I never knew you: depart from me, ye that work iniquity."

1 John 4:1: "Beloved, believe not every spirit, but try the spirits whether they are of God: because many false prophets are gone out into the world."

Not All Who Say, "Thus Saith the Lord," Are Speaking the Word of the Lord

When I was a new Christian, I learned this lesson very well—that not everyone who says, "Thus saith the Lord," is really speaking the word of the Lord.

God had spoken to my heart and my wife Karen's heart, to go to Bible college. After a three-week mini-mission to Mexico, we were preparing to move to Mt. Vernon, Ohio, the location of the Bible college. A woman, who was a so-called prophetess and did not know what the Lord had already clearly spoken to Karen and me, prophesied over us during a service, saying we were to go back to Mexico.

I said, "I'm still a relatively new Christian and I am not that mature in the Lord. I don't know the Word very well yet, but I do know that if God told me to go to Bible college, if God told me to buy a mobile home, if God enabled us to find the very last mobile home lot on which we could put our mobile home in the city where we were to move, then God wants me there. And that's where I'm going!"

I had to decide: Do I follow the voice of someone telling me God's will for my life, or do I follow God's Word and what His Spirit has led me to do? I chose to follow the Lord, and many times since, I have reflected back on how disastrous my life and ministry would have been had I not followed His direction during that crucial decision in my life. But because I obeyed God's voice, He has produced tremendous fruit through our ministry, done the impossible through our lives, and honored and blessed us greatly. This woman, who people exalted and almost deified, eventually fell away from the Lord.

In a tragic story in 1 Kings 13, we see that the word of the

Lord came to a man of God and told him what he was to do. In obedience he began to follow the word of the Lord, but when a false prophet told him something contrary to what God had already told him to do, he obeyed that prophet. As a result of obeying the deceiving prophet, and thereby disobeying the Lord, the man was killed by a lion that very day.

The message is crystal clear: when God speaks to you, obey! If what God says contradicts what a prophet says, then follow the word of the Lord and do not follow that prophet.

God wants you to obey His voice and His Word. Develop that relationship with Him, and do not give responsibility to any supposed prophet or anyone who prophesies over you. It is between you and the Lord. (For background information and context read 1 Kings 11:43 through 12:33, as well as all of 1 Kings 13.)

False Leaders Use Control and Manipulation

It is both dangerous and diabolical that some use "Thus saith the Lord" to control and manipulate people. One of many illustrations I could cite concerns a young man who called me because he was very confused about the teaching he was receiving in church from his pastor. He wanted to leave this church, but his pastor said: "Thus saith the Lord, if you leave, one of your children will die." Needless to say, he was terrorized and afraid to leave.

Think about some of the prophecies today in light of what Peter said, "But there were false prophets also among the people, even as there shall be false teachers among you, who privily shall bring in damnable heresies, even denying the Lord that bought them, and bring upon themselves swift destruction. And many shall follow their pernicious ways; by reason of whom the way of truth shall be evil spoken of. And through covetousness shall they with feigned words make merchandise of you: whose judgment now of a long time lingereth not, and their damnation slumbereth not" (2 Peter 2:1–3).

Tell Me God's Will for My Life

When I was a new Christian, people tried to tell me what the Lord wanted me to do. As I matured in the Lord, they wanted me to tell them God's will for their lives. I won't have any part of either one. I will share the Word and what the Holy Spirit impresses on my heart and pray for them, but the final responsibility concerning God's direction for one's life lies between God and that individual.

I remember when I was a brand-new Christian. I went to a man of God whom I greatly respected. I said, "You are so close to the Lord, He speaks to you so much. Would you pray and tell me what God wants me to do?" It was a cop-out. I wanted a quick, easy, convenient way to get God's guidance. He said, "Bill, it is your responsibility to seek God's will for your life. You had better learn right now to discipline yourself to get into God's Word and get on your knees to seek God's will and know His voice." And although I was at first disappointed, he taught me a very crucial biblical principle.

In John 10:27, Jesus said, "My sheep hear my voice, and I know them, and they follow me." We need to hear and know Jesus' voice.

If we are not on speaking terms with the Lord—so that He has to speak to someone else to tell us what to do—then we had better repent. We better discipline ourselves before the Lord and get into His Word and seek Him through prayer and fasting (as the true prophets in the Bible did) so we too can hear His voice.

The Supernatural and Spectacular Are Not the Usual

Many think those who are seemingly having frequent audible voices, visions, personal prophecies, revelations, and words from the Lord are super-spiritual. But I wonder where their hearts are before the Lord. Are they hardhearted and insensitive to His Spirit? Are they undisciplined to read His Word and to pray? Is the use of the spectacular the only way He can get them to hear His voice and obey?

I would rather be so sensitive and surrendered to the Lord that He can speak to my heart through His Word and Spirit—without always having to do something phenomenal to get my attention, or without having to send some prophet to get my life in order or to tell me what to do. Usually in the case of hardheartedness, such as Baalam when God spoke through a donkey, or for special situations like Moses at the burning bush when He called him to lead the children of Israel out of Egyptian bondage, or when God gave Peter a vision to do something "unthinkable" (take the Gospel to the Gentiles), did God resort to supernatural, spectacular ways of revealing His will.

Prophets Are Not Our "Guides"

Donald Gee writes in his book, *Concerning Spiritual Gifts:*

> There are no indications in the New Testament that it is the function of prophets in the church to be her guides in the sense that they guided Israel of old—by a system of "inquiring of the Lord." There are indeed instances such as the prophecy of Agabus concerning the forthcoming famine (Acts 11:28), or the fate of Paul at Jerusalem (Acts

21:11), where the prophet plainly foretells what may happen. But it is significant that he offers no guidance; it is left to the individual members of the church to determine… (Acts 11:29) what they would do, and to Paul to decide his own course of action (Acts 21:13).

Still more significant is the fact that there is no attempt to use the gift of prophecy or the office of prophet in the great dispute that arose about circumcision in Acts 15; or in Paul's obvious personal dilemma as to the next step for his ministry in Acts 16:6–10, though on both occasions Silas, a recognized "prophet" (15:32), was on the spot.

It can truthfully be affirmed that there is not one single instance of the gift of prophecy being deliberately resorted to for guidance in the New Testament.[9]

Even though there are prophets and prophecy in the New Testament, these are not the same as they were in the Old Testament. In the Old Testament the prophet was often like Moses or Samuel who was the recognized spokesman, not only for God to the people, but for the people to the Lord. He was the mediator. In the New Testament, when Jesus died on the cross, the curtain in the temple—separating the Holy Place from the Holy of Holies—was torn in two from top to bottom (Matthew 27:51). Through Christ, our Mediator, we now have direct access to the presence of God.

There is also another aspect in the New Testament to consider—Pentecost. Now all believers can be filled with God's Spirit and be personally led by the Spirit of God. We have the promise of Romans 8:14, "For as many as are led by the Spirit of God, they are the sons of God."

Bonds and Afflictions Await Paul

The account of the prophecy by Agabus, that Paul would be bound in Jerusalem, is often inaccurately used to validate guidance through personal prophecy. Looking at this account in Scriptural context reveals a different conclusion.

First, we discover that before Agabus prophesied, Paul already knew from the Holy Spirit that bonds and afflictions awaited him. Acts 20:22, 23 says: "And now, behold, I go bound in the spirit unto Jerusalem, not knowing the things that shall befall me there: Save that the Holy Ghost witnesseth in every city, saying that bonds and afflictions abide me."

Acts 21:4 repeats this: "And finding disciples, we tarried there seven days: who said to Paul through the Spirit, that he should not go up to Jerusalem."

Then in Acts 21:10–14, Agabus confirms:

And as we tarried there many days, there came down from Judaea a certain prophet, named Agabus. And when he was come unto us, he took Paul's girdle, and bound his own hands and feet, and said, Thus saith the Holy Ghost, So shall the Jews at Jerusalem bind the man that owneth this girdle, and shall deliver him into the hands of the Gentiles. And when we heard these things, both we, and they of that place, besought him not to go up to Jerusalem. Then Paul answered, What mean ye to weep and to break mine heart? for I am ready not to be bound only, but also to die at Jerusalem for the name of the Lord Jesus. And when he would not be persuaded, we ceased, saying, The will of the Lord be done.

The prophet Agabus merely told Paul what was going to happen. It was Paul's responsibility to determine what he would do. We need to keep that Scriptural balance in mind.

After Paul spoke to the Sanhedrin in Jerusalem, the Lord once again confirmed that it was His leading for Paul to go to Jerusalem, for He said to the apostle in Acts 23:11, "And the night following the Lord stood by him, and said, Be of good cheer, Paul: for as thou hast testified of me in Jerusalem, so must thou bear witness also at Rome."

Prophets and Personal Prophecy Book

The owner of a Christian bookstore asked me to review a leading book on the topic of prophets and personal prophecy. I gave it to our research director, and after only twenty minutes of checking, he said it was heresy. Next, I gave it to a biblical apologist who said it was unscriptural. Then I gave it to an Assemblies of God pastor who is very knowledgeable of Scripture, and he said the foundation principles of it were built on sand. Finally, I read it myself and confirmed the book was in error.

My basic conclusion after reading this book is that the author has deviated from the truth in three ways:

1) He has taken the Scriptural promises and blessings that are for those who have faith and obedience in the Lord and His Word and reinterpreted them to be for those who have faith and obedience in prophets and personal prophecy. A very subtle transition occurs much in the same way Satan subtly changed God's Word as he tempted people in Scripture.

2) He has reinterpreted and taken out of Scriptural context almost every Scripture that refers directly or indirectly to prophets and personal prophecy, trying to justify his emphasis on multitudes of personal prophecies.

3) He is teaching "Christian fortune-telling" rather than the biblical operation of prophecy.

Scripture-twisting

Many people who profess to love the Lord are caught up in this twisting of Scripture. Christian leaders and those who claim to be prophets use this book (and similar books) as their source for prophetic guidelines. I wonder where their discernment is. If they really have the Holy Spirit, why does He not speak to their hearts? If they know God's Word, why do they not see how Scripture is being twisted?

Over and over as I read or listened to materials by those endorsing personal prophecy, the Scriptures were taken out of context, the meanings were twisted, and the Scripture references given were often totally unrelated to the unscriptural conclusions they made. It was the same Scripture-twisting tactics used by many cults to lure those with little Bible knowledge, and who lack the time or motivation to search Scripture, to blindly follow their beliefs and practices.

Control and Manipulation

Leaders of a discipleship movement supposedly repented of the "wrong and injurious" extremes and the "unhealthy submission resulting in perverse and unbiblical obedience to human leaders."[10] But something very similar and even more sinister is occurring through many supposed prophets and personal prophecies.

A woman from Florida, a charismatic believer who is constantly in the Word, went to a church affiliated with the prophets. She said as soon as she walked in, she knew in her spirit something was wrong. Not only did they give an incorrect prophecy concerning her, but also she said, "The people were controlled by the prophets and prophetesses in the church."

It was the "spirit of shepherding and discipleship" manifest through the so-called prophets. It was the same control and manipulation, the same replacing of the Holy Spirit and Christ's Lordship with human beings whom we look to for decisions and guidance.

How accurate Jeremiah was for today when he said: "A wonderful and horrible thing is committed in the land; The prophets prophesy falsely, and the priests bear rule by their means; and my people love to have it so: and what will ye do in the end thereof?" (Jeremiah 5:30, 31).

It is interesting that many of these so-called prophets only seem to prophesy flattery and great things for their associates. However, they often resort to a form of "black witchcraft" by mainly prophesying doom and destruction against those who disagree or oppose them.

I wondered why a so-called prophet of God did not detect and rebuke the spirit of deceit and occultism in a church where he frequently spoke. Instead, he prophesied blessing and that everything was right on course before the Lord.

I soon discovered he spoke from his own inspiration, and he always had such positive words of blessing and prosperity because this church was supporting him financially. It reminds me of Micah 3:11 which says, "the prophets thereof divine for money…"

Nehemiah 6:10–14 records:

> Afterward I came unto the house of Shemaiah the son of Delaiah the son of Mehetabeel, who was shut up; and he said, Let us meet together in the house of God, within the temple, and let us shut the doors of the temple: for they will come to slay thee; yea, in the night will they come to slay thee. And I said, Should such a man as I flee? and who is there, that, being as I am, would go into the temple to save his life? I will not go in. And, lo, I perceived that God had not sent him; but that he pronounced this prophecy against me: for Tobiah and Sanballat had hired him. Therefore was he hired, that I should be afraid, and do so, and sin, and that they might have matter for an evil report, that they might reproach me. My God, think thou upon Tobiah and Sanballat according to these their works, and on the prophetess Noadiah, and the rest of the prophets, that would have put me in fear.

Demonically Inspired Prophecies

Shortly after confronting the pastor who motivated the writing of my initial *Beware* booklet, a prophecy proclaiming his vindication and victory, followed by a prophecy for my immediate destruction, were given at a pastors' conference he attended hosting two "prophets."

These demonically-inspired prophecies sounded so close to the truth—but in reality were so far away. If only those pastors had genuine discernment and went by the Word, they would not have been deceived. But they trusted in false prophets and false prophecies, which proved to be stepping-stones to even greater deception.

It was because of the pastors and "apostles" acceptance, tolerance, and endorsement of these prophecies and this pastor that enabled him to continue spiritually raping many more people until he was undeniably exposed in a scandal that devastated his church and family.

The prophecy of my doom indicated it would be just like Korah received for opposing Moses. But it was fatally flawed. First, Moses challenged Korah and his accomplices to meet with him the next day to let the Lord decide (Numbers 16), but this pastor and his cohorts were afraid and unwilling to meet with me.

Second, in Scripture, God sent prophets to deliver warnings prior to His judgment, but these "prophets," pastors, and "apostles" did not have the courage to even warn me about the prophecy of my impending destruction. They would not even give me a copy of the recorded prophecy. It was not until five years later that I finally was given a copy—only because a woman who could no longer tolerate the unbiblical nonsense and left the church gave it to me.

Third, Korah's judgment was meted out swiftly as the earth opened up and swallowed him, Dathan, Abiram, and their households (Numbers 16). The prophecy of my imminent destruction proved to be completely wrong as the Lord protected me in numerous extremely dangerous situations during overseas mission outreaches and empowered and anointed me as the ministry continued to grow internationally. It was the pastor who received prophecies for blessing and victory that was "destroyed." And several of the ones who so vehemently opposed me experienced physical and spiritual devastation.

As the years passed, the error of their ways and the resulting disastrous consequences became visible. The credibility and integrity of my life and ministry was enhanced as the test of time proved the truth of God's Word and the faithfulness of the God whom I serve.

Reflecting back on how his brothers sold him as a slave into Egypt and the Lord turned it around for good, Joseph said to his brothers, "But as for you, ye thought evil against me; but God meant it unto good" (Genesis 50:20).

We read in Exodus 10:28, 29: "And Pharaoh said unto him, Get thee from me, take heed to thyself, see my face no more; for in that day thou seest my face thou shalt die. And Moses said, Thou hast spoken well, I will see thy face again no more."

But it did not happen the way Pharaoh expected. Neither did the prophecy for my destruction turn out as that pastor and his associates had hoped. And it did not happen the way Haman anticipated. Esther 9:24, 25 explains: "Because Haman the son of Hammedatha, the Agagite, the enemy of all the Jews, had devised against the Jews to destroy them, and had cast Pur, that is, the lot, to consume them, and to destroy them; But when Esther came before the king, he commanded by letters that his wicked device, which he devised against the Jews, should return upon his own head, and that he and his sons should be hanged on the gallows."

1 Kings 22:20–23 says: "And the LORD said, Who shall persuade Ahab, that he may go up and fall at Ramothgilead? And one said on this manner, and another said on that manner. And there came forth a spirit, and stood before the LORD, and said, I will persuade him. And the LORD said unto him, Wherewith?

And he said, I will go forth, and I will be a lying spirit in the mouth of all his prophets. And he said, Thou shalt persuade him, and prevail also: go forth, and do so. Now therefore, behold, the LORD hath put a lying spirit in the mouth of all these thy prophets, and the LORD hath spoken evil concerning thee."

In the same way as the preceding Scripture, the Lord showed me that He allowed that false prophecy so that those pastors would have a false assurance and security and boldly align themselves with this other pastor, thus exposing their true beliefs and eventually causing their own words to bring God's judgment on themselves.

Who Would You Believe?

The opposition and prophecy about my destruction came from people who were supposed prophets, apostles, and pastors who:

- had foundational beliefs about prophecy which are built on error and Scripture-twisting;
- made unscriptural excuses for not being 100 percent accurate;
- and propagated unbiblical teachings, practices, and phenomena.

The leading "apostle" announced from his pulpit prior to the prophecy for my destruction that the Lord had "led him to build his new church like Bill Rudge built his ministry center, on total faith without any interest or loans," but months later when his "word from the Lord" was proven inaccurate he asked for anyone who had a word of direction from the Lord to let him know.

Should I have believed them? Or should I believe the Word of God and the Spirit of God? In over thirty years of ministry, the Lord has fulfilled 100 percent of what I have publicly proclaimed that He has led me to do, much of which seemed totally impossible. But God has been faithful—and the end result has always been ultimate victory!

I think the spirit from which these supposed prophets prophesied is evident. It is the same spirit I have encountered over the years in dealing with many occultists. It is the same spirit that motivated someone from one of their churches to actually team up with a leading occultist and attempt to destroy our ministry. It is the same spirit that during this time spoke as a demon in a woman's dream telling her to destroy our ministry and telling her husband (in her dream) to kill me.

I may one day die for Christ, but the Lord has assured me that my life will not be taken until His purpose is fulfilled. My prayer is: "Lord, let me have the grace, the power, the boldness, and the forgiving attitude of Your servant Stephen." (See Acts 6:8–7:60.)

The Final Test

The final test that proves who really heard from God is the end result. In Scripture, there are several instances where a false prophet opposed and attempted to undermine and discredit a true prophet of God. But in the end, God always vindicated and honored His true messenger.

Jeremiah 28:10–17 states:

Then Hananiah the prophet took the yoke from off the prophet Jeremiah's neck, and brake it. And Hananiah spake in the presence of all the people, saying, Thus saith the LORD; Even so will I break the yoke of Nebuchadnezzar king of Babylon from the neck of all nations within the space of two full years. And the prophet Jeremiah went his way. Then the word of the LORD came unto Jeremiah the prophet, after that Hananiah the prophet had broken the yoke from off the neck of the prophet Jeremiah, saying, Go and tell Hananiah, saying, Thus saith the LORD; Thou hast broken the yokes of wood; but thou shalt make for them yokes of iron. For thus saith the LORD of hosts, the God of Israel; I have put a yoke of iron upon the neck of all these nations, that they may serve Nebuchadnezzar king of Babylon; and they shall serve him: and I have given him the beasts of the field also. Then said the prophet Jeremiah unto Hananiah the prophet, Hear now, Hananiah; The LORD hath not sent thee; but thou makest this people to trust in a lie. Therefore thus saith the LORD; Behold, I will cast thee from off the face of the earth: this year thou shalt die, because thou hast taught rebellion against the LORD. So Hananiah the prophet died the same year in the seventh month.

On another occasion, Jeremiah was beaten and put in stocks at the order of the priest Pashur, chief officer in the temple (Jeremiah 20:1, 2), because Jeremiah had pronounced God's upcoming judgment on Jerusalem (Jeremiah 19:15). When Jeremiah was released, the Lord again proclaimed through him judgment on Jerusalem and Judah (Jeremiah 20:3–5). And then Jeremiah prophesied to Pashur: "And thou, Pashur, and all that dwell in thine house shall go into captivity: and thou shalt come to Babylon, and there thou shalt die, and shalt be buried there, thou, and all thy friends, to whom thou hast prophesied lies" (Jeremiah 20:6).

After Jeremiah's release from a dungeon in which he would have surely died, and later his rescue from a cistern in which he would have starved to death, he prophesied to King Zedekiah: "But if thou wilt not go forth to the king of Babylon's princes, then shall this city be given into the hand of the Chaldeans, and they shall burn it with fire, and thou shalt not escape out of their hand" (Jeremiah 38:18).

We see the tragic fulfillment of this prophecy in Jeremiah, chapter 39.

False Peace vs. Impending Judgment

Even though Jeremiah's prophecies of the people being taken into captivity from Jerusalem to Babylon were being fulfilled, Ahab and Zedekiah, two false prophets, continued to prophesy lies. As a result, they were burned in Nebuchadnezzar's fire—not spared like Shadrach, Meshach, and Abednego. Jeremiah 29:20–23 gives the following account of these two false prophets:

> Hear ye therefore the word of the LORD, all ye of the captivity, whom I have sent from Jerusalem to Babylon: Thus saith the LORD of hosts, the God of Israel, of Ahab the son of Kolaiah, and of Zedekiah the son of Maaseiah, which prophesy a lie unto you in my name; Behold, I will deliver them into the hand of Nebuchadrezzar king of Babylon; and he shall slay them before your eyes; And of them shall be taken up a curse by all the captivity of Judah which are in Babylon, saying, The LORD make

thee like Zedekiah and like Ahab, whom the king of Babylon roasted in the fire; Because they have committed villany in Israel, and have committed adultery with their neighbours' wives, and have spoken lying words in my name, which I have not commanded them; even I know, and am a witness, saith the LORD.

Occasionally the Lord has led me to caution or warn individuals or groups concerning unscriptural teachings and practices they are propagating. And after a time of much prayer, fasting, Scripture study, and examining my heart and motives, I would do so. As I look back over the years, I am amazed and humbled that all those who refused to repent have become even more perverse in their teachings and practices and have eventually suffered the consequences.

I have seen the false teachings and the false prophets come and go. I can somewhat relate to Jeremiah, who after faithfully proclaiming God's Word for many years, questioned King Zedekiah regarding the false prophets: "Where are now your prophets which prophesied unto you, saying, The king of Babylon shall not come against you, nor against this land?" (Jeremiah 37:19).

Similar to the false prophets of Jeremiah's day who were prophesying peace and prosperity, today's "prophets" continually prophesy renewal, revival, and restoration. But is much of the "revival" occurring today really a commitment to the Christ of the Bible and biblical Christianity, or is it merely an attraction to all the excitement and phenomena going on?

Jeremiah accurately prophesied God's impending judgment because of the many sins of the people and their leaders. Then— in contrast to the false peace of the false prophets—Jeremiah prophesied the Lord's promised restoration (Jeremiah 33).

When the judgment prophesied by Jeremiah finally comes upon Judah and Jerusalem, he records his deep distress in the book of Lamentations, which clearly shows the consequences of sin and apostasy.

Lamentations 2:2–5 states:

The LORD hath swallowed up all the habitations of Jacob, and hath not pitied: he hath thrown down in his wrath the strong holds of the daughter of Judah; he hath brought them down to the ground: he hath polluted the kingdom and the princes thereof. He hath cut off in his fierce anger all the horn of Israel: he hath drawn back his right hand from before the enemy, and he burned against Jacob like a flaming fire, which devoureth round about. He hath bent his bow like an enemy: he stood with his right hand as an adversary, and slew all that were pleasant to the eye in the tabernacle of the daughter of Zion: he poured out his fury like fire. The LORD was as an enemy: he hath swallowed up Israel, he hath swallowed up all her palaces: he hath destroyed his strong holds, and hath increased in the daughter of Judah mourning and lamentation

Lamentations 4:12, 13: "The kings of the earth, and all the inhabitants of the world, would not have believed that the adversary and the enemy should have entered into the gates of Jerusalem. For the sins of her prophets, and the iniquities of her priests, that have shed the blood of the just in the midst of her."

I believe Scripture strongly indicates a similar end-time scenario of God's judgment on an apostate church and rebellious world (tribulation period), and then Christ's Second Coming and promised restoration of all things.

Lamentations speaks of that hope of restoration in the following verses:

Lamentations 3:21–26, 40: "This I recall to my mind, therefore have I hope. It is of the LORD's mercies that we are not consumed, because his compassions fail not. They are new every morning: great is thy faithfulness. The LORD is my portion, saith my soul; therefore will I hope in him. The LORD is good unto them that wait for him, to the soul that seeketh him. It is good that a man should both hope and quietly wait for the salvation of the LORD. Let us search and try our ways, and turn again to the LORD."

Just as Jeremiah suffered and was persecuted for his obedient testimony for God and for speaking the true word of the Lord, so too, true believers who remain faithful will greatly suffer because of their testimony for Jesus (the Jesus of the Bible) and the Word of God. In fact, no less than five times does Revelation (in regards to the Apostle John or the persecution of end-time believers who refuse to compromise) mention the utterly crucial and central nature of the Word of God and their testimony for Jesus (Revelation 1:2; 1:9; 6:9; 12:17; 20:4).

A "Spirit" Comes on These People

A "spirit" seems to come on these people once they submit to these false prophets and their false prophecies and teachings. I have seen several that, after being confronted with the truth yet choosing to continue involvement in a group or church propagating these errors, had a visible countenance change and their hearts became hardened.

These people are being taught a "Christianized fortune-telling." This happened to a woman I knew who had a gentle, loving spirit. She attended one of these "prophets' schools," and after submitting to that teaching immediately began to manifest a spirit of haughtiness and rebellion.

She refused to sit down with me and go through the Scriptures on prophets and personal prophecy or attend a lecture I was giving on the topic, even though I offered her an opportunity to respond. And this woman, who previously (when I was in her favor) had given an unconditional prophecy of blessing for my life and ministry, as well as future persecution, now started prophesying my destruction, and ended up becoming so deceived and vengeful that she became part of that very persecution. Unlike the prophet Nathan who confronted David and prophesied to his face (2 Samuel 12:1–14), this supposed prophet (and many others like her) cowardly prophesied my destruction to other people behind my back.

On another occasion a traveling "prophet" stopped by our ministry center. He said the Lord led him to me. After a few minutes of cordial conversation, I informed him that I believed that he and those to whom he was submitted were not speaking the words of the Lord, but were into "Christianized fortune-telling" and speaking from their own inspiration and a counterfeit spirit.

He became irate and said I was young and inexperienced. As he stood up he informed me he was going to prophesy my destruction—thinking I would be intimidated. I said, "Go ahead and prophesy my destruction. But I want to let you know that when you are done, I am going to pray the Lord gives you a double portion of what you prophesy. And then we will see whose prophecy is fulfilled!" He refused to prophesy in my presence, but hurried out of the ministry center. As he pulled away in his motor home, he threw garbage in our parking lot.

Vague Prophecies

Much of what is being accepted as genuine prophecy today is unscriptural nonsense and is being given by those who are speaking from their own inspiration or a demonic counterfeit.

Most of the prophecies I hear today are unimpressive, powerless, and inaccurate. They are more like psychic readings or fortune-telling than biblical prophecy. Many are "safe prophecies"—so vague and general that they could be true of almost anyone, like those found in fortune cookies.

In contrast, prophecies recorded in Scripture were almost always very specific. Some were fulfilled almost immediately and others were not fulfilled for years or even centuries, but they were precise and exact.

For example: "And Joshua adjured them at that time, saying, Cursed be the man before the LORD, that riseth up and buildeth this city Jericho: he shall lay the foundation thereof in his firstborn, and in his youngest son shall he set up the gates of it" (Joshua 6:26).

This specific prophecy was fulfilled generations later: "In his days did Hiel the Bethelite build Jericho: he laid the foundation thereof in Abiram his firstborn, and set up the gates thereof in his youngest son Segub, according to the word of the LORD, which he spake by Joshua the son of Nun" (1 Kings 16:34).

Donald C. Stamps, general editor of *The Full Life Study Bible* stated: "Many of Jeremiah's prophecies were fulfilled in his own lifetime (e.g., Jeremiah 16:9; 20:4; 25:1–14; 27:19–22; 28:15–17; 34:1–5); other prophecies involving the far-distant future were fulfilled later or are yet to be fulfilled (e.g., 23:5–6; 30:8–9; 31:31–34; 33:14–16)."[11]

Obedience Prophecies

There are prophecies in Scripture where blessings are promised if the word of the Lord is obeyed. Adverse consequences are promised if it is not obeyed.

Isaiah 1:19, 20 states: "If ye be willing and obedient, ye shall eat the good of the land: But if ye refuse and rebel, ye shall be devoured with the sword: for the mouth of the LORD hath spoken it."

The prophet Jeremiah gave King Zedekiah a choice. If he would obey the word of the Lord and surrender to the King of Babylon, his life would be spared, his family would live, and Jerusalem would not be burned. But if Zedekiah did not obey, then Jerusalem would be handed over to the Babylonians and burned with fire and he would not escape (Jeremiah 38:17, 18).

There is a similar prophecy in Jeremiah 42:8–18, which was given to the remnant left in Israel after the Babylonian captivity. They were told that if they stayed in the land, they would be blessed, but if they went to Egypt to reside there they would die by the sword, famine, and plague.

A Call to Repentance

Many prophecies were a call to repentance, such as Isaiah 58:1: "Cry aloud, spare not, lift up thy voice like a trumpet, and show my people their transgression, and the house of Jacob their sins."

Joel 2:12–14 states: "Therefore also now, saith the LORD, turn ye even to me with all your heart, and with fasting, and with weeping, and with mourning: And rend your heart, and not your garments, and turn unto the LORD your God: for he is gracious and merciful, slow to anger, and of great kindness, and repenteth him of the evil. Who knoweth if he will return and repent, and leave a blessing behind him; even a meat offering and a drink offering unto the LORD your God?"

Jonah 1:1, 2 commands: "Now the word of the LORD came unto Jonah the son of Amittai, saying, Arise, go to Nineveh, that great city, and cry against it; for their wickedness is come up before me."

Zechariah 7:8–14 admonishes:

And the word of the LORD came unto Zechariah, saying, Thus speaketh the LORD of hosts, saying, Execute true judgment, and shew mercy and compassions every man to his brother: And oppress not the widow, nor the fatherless, the stranger, nor the poor; and let none of you imagine evil against his brother in your heart. But they refused to hearken, and pulled away the shoulder, and stopped their ears, that they should not hear. Yea, they made their hearts as an adamant stone, lest they should hear the law, and the words which the LORD of hosts hath sent in his spirit by the former prophets: therefore came a great wrath from the LORD of hosts. Therefore it is come to pass, that as he cried, and they would not hear; so they cried, and I would not hear, saith the LORD of hosts: But I scattered them with a whirlwind among all the nations whom they knew not. Thus the land was desolate after them, that no man passed through nor returned: for they laid the pleasant land desolate.

Prophecies Must Be 100 Percent Accurate

Not only are most prophecies today usually very vague and general, they are rarely 100 percent accurate. Many rise up and proclaim: "God told me to say this. God said to go here or to do this. God showed me this is going to happen." But it doesn't come to pass. If a few of their prophecies are fulfilled, these are used to give them credibility, while the prophecies which were proved false are ignored or altered to conform to the circumstances.

Many supposed prophets attempt to whitewash the fact that they are not 100 percent accurate by stating something like: "A prophet is not a false prophet simply because something he/she says is inaccurate or doesn't seem to apply to us. The prophet may be honest, righteous, and upright, yet immature in his prophesying. Missing it a few times doesn't make one a false prophet. If it did, most preachers and teachers would do best to cease ministering as well." But that is not Scriptural. Biblical prophecies were amazingly accurate. Prophecies of impending judgment were fulfilled unless the people repented (1 Kings 21:27–29; Isaiah 38:1–8; Jeremiah 18:7–10, 26:2–6, 12, 13; Jonah 3:1–10). Promises were not revoked unless the people were disobedient (1 Samuel 2:30).

Although Hananiah, the *false* prophet was not accurate, Jeremiah the *true* prophet was. Jeremiah 28:15–17 says: "Then said the prophet Jeremiah unto Hananiah the prophet, Hear now, Hananiah; The LORD hath not sent thee; but thou makest this people to trust in a lie. Therefore thus saith the LORD; Behold, I will cast thee from off the face of the earth: this year thou shalt die, because thou hast taught rebellion against the LORD. So Hananiah the prophet died the same year in the seventh month."

Countless prophecies in Scripture validate this type of accuracy in prophecy—not to mention the amazing fulfillment of specific Messianic prophecies. When a prophet saying, "Thus saith the Lord," is inaccurate, he had better repent. There is a tremendous difference between a pastor sharing his insight of Scripture or a counselor saying, "This is my opinion of what you should do," or "This is the biblical counsel and advice for your situation," and someone saying, "Thus saith the Lord" or "This is God's word to you."

Deuteronomy 18:21, 22 states: "And if thou say in thine heart, How shall we know the word which the LORD hath not spoken? When a prophet speaketh in the name of the LORD, if the thing follow not, nor come to pass, that is the thing which the LORD hath not spoken, but the prophet hath spoken it presumptuously: thou shalt not be afraid of him."

Now if we practiced what they did in Old Testament times to false prophets, we would not have so many going around saying, "Thus saith the Lord." For Deuteronomy 18:20 warns: "But the prophet, which shall presume to speak a word in my name, which I have not commanded him to speak, or that shall speak in the name of other gods, even that prophet shall die."

Those who prophesy from their own inspiration will never be 100 percent accurate unless they merely give general and vague prophecies. Satan is not omniscient and therefore not 100 percent accurate, which is why so many of the predictions from those who prophesy through demonic inspiration do not come to pass either.

Isaiah 44:24, 25 reveals: "Thus saith the LORD, thy redeemer, and he that formed thee from the womb, I am the LORD that maketh all things; that stretcheth forth the heavens alone; that spreadeth abroad the earth by myself; That frustrateth the tokens of the liars, and maketh diviners mad; that turneth wise men backward, and maketh their knowledge foolish."

In contrast, Scripture says regarding Samuel, one of God's true prophets: "And Samuel grew, and the LORD was with him, and did let none of his words fall to the ground. And all Israel from Dan even to Beersheba knew that Samuel was established to be a prophet of the LORD" (1 Samuel 3:19, 20).

1 Samuel 9:6 states: "And he said unto him, Behold now, there is in this city a man of God, and he is an honourable man; all that he saith cometh surely to pass: now let us go thither; peradventure he can shew us our way that we should go."

New Age Channelers

I believe Satan raises up certain people and gives them false prophecies, dreams, and visions to depreciate those who genuinely hear from the Lord.

While trance-channelers communicate New Age beliefs from the spirits, many so-called prophets of God do exactly the same thing. They have become channels for deceiving spirits whose revelations are often amazingly similar to New Age teaching.

After I spoke at a church, a man told me God was continually speaking to him. But the prophecies and revelations "this voice" was giving him were completely contrary to Scripture. If adhered to, they would actually lead Christians to accept the reign of Antichrist and be part of the prophesied apostasy.

I asked him, "What is the proof that you are really hearing from God? What Scriptural validation can you provide? What specific fulfillments have occurred?" I explained to him that, "Whenever I have said the Lord has spoken to me, I can substantiate it by God's Word and it has always been fulfilled." He had neither proof yet he wanted to persuade me that his revelations were from God.

Even more tragic than his personal delusion was the fact that he was attempting to influence a church, and if possible, believers throughout the U.S. I told him he needed to renounce "this voice" that was speaking to him—for it was lying, and deceiving him.

There are countless people like him who are claiming revelations, dreams, visions, and prophecies from God. Most are mere human imagination while some are demonic spirits. Most are not only extra-biblical, but contrary to Scripture. Most have no validation of fulfillment to even consider they might be from God.

Inaccurate prophecies and unbiblical revelations are used by the enemy to discredit biblical prophecy, and undermine what God is truly speaking by His Spirit.

It's More Like Fortune-Telling

I have researched many psychics and fortune-tellers, and there seems to be no apparent difference between their method of prediction and degree of accuracy and that of many so-called prophets of God today. The only difference, seemingly, is that the supposed prophet often uses "Thus saith the Lord."

At a meeting where "holy laughter" was occurring, a woman stood up to give a prophetic utterance. For several minutes she rambled on to the enthusiastic receptivity of the pastor and audience. She called out many ailments that God was supposedly healing (most of which could be true for almost anyone in the audience) and none of which were documented as being healed. It sounded more like a psychic reading than biblical prophecy. She also shared for several minutes about the revelation Jesus was supposedly giving her that everyone in the room was being encompassed by light. I thought I was at a New Age gathering—not a Spirit-filled church. When she finished, those in attendance applauded.

One pastor, also known as an apostle, announced at his church that a woman prophetess was coming next week, so he invited everyone to come back for a personal prophecy. They might as well go to the local fortune-teller or psychic.

Biblical prophets did not prophesy at will, but when the word of the Lord came to them. Jeremiah 42:7 states, "And it came to pass after ten days, that the word of the LORD came unto Jeremiah." New Testament prophecy also was not determined by the whims of the person operating the gift, but as the Spirit gave utterance.

I saw the following ad in a Christian magazine: "For your personal prophecy send your name, address, and love offering." This resembles fortune-telling far more than any form of prophecy in the Bible.

I frequently saw a large "Palm Reader" sign in the front yard of a house, and then one day, I noticed the sign was replaced by a new sign that read, "Christian Advisor—Advice on All Matters." Will it next be changed to "Christian Prophet"?

This person probably discovered that there is a gullible market of Christians who do not want to get on their knees and into God's Word to seek His will for their lives.

I was later informed that some Christians helped her change the sign. I hope it was a genuine conversion, but I have my doubts.

It was merely a change of terminology. Even if she was converted, she had no business setting herself up that fast as a Christian consultant without time to grow and mature in the Lord.

Meetings where prophets have people line up or call them out and give them a word from the Lord, or meetings where everybody is prophesying over each other, resemble many of the occult and New Age meetings I have researched.

With this in mind, it doesn't surprise me that a supposed prophet of God who was giving personal prophecies at churches throughout the country stated that his wife was "at a women's meeting one day and God got hold of her and picked her up out of the chair, supernaturally, and threw her on the floor and she was jerking; she couldn't stop her jerk..."

I have encountered accounts like this in the occult through demonic phenomena, but never of true believers in Scripture.

Putting Personal Prophecies Above God's Word

Although most deny it, the sad reality is that many put the personal prophecies they receive above God's Word. They are encouraged to get a recorded copy of their personal prophecies and write them out and meditate on them and read or listen to them repeatedly.

One noted prophet stated he follows his prophet mentor without question. "Whatever he tells me to do, I do it. I am not into shepherding. I am under protection; I have a covering." He may have a covering from that supposed prophet, but he has removed himself from under the Lordship of Jesus Christ.

Deuteronomy 13:1–5 makes known that even if their prophecies come to pass—if they cause you to follow other gods, *they are false prophets*. At first I thought, "These prophets are not making anyone go after other gods. They appear to glorify Jesus Christ." But, as I sought the Lord and His Word and researched more, I discovered that their prophecies were getting further and further away from biblical Christianity. In too many cases they are causing people to go after other gods. They are subtly removing the God of the Bible and Christ's Lordship from their followers' lives and making them dependent on the prophet. They are also replacing the Word of God by encouraging the people to obey, memorize, and conform to personal prophecies and "new revelations."

So-called prophets of God have prophesied over many separated or divorced people that their spouse would come back to them. Some of these people have waited years. Some even wait for the fulfillment of the prophecy after their former spouse has married someone else—making it unscriptural for them to reunite (Deuteronomy 24:4).

There is a growing number of casualties—people who have been hurt, confused, and misled by supposed prophets and prophetic utterances. Many of these victims have been spiritually inoculated and now want nothing to do with the real Jesus of the Bible.

Cult Awareness on "New Revelations"

It is sad to discover that what I had written many years ago about the cults concerning "new revelations" is relevant for the Church today. The following excerpts are from my former *Cult Awareness* booklet:

Although they say their "new revelation" merely sheds additional light on what God has already revealed through the Scriptures, in reality, it adds to or subtracts from the Bible. Ultimately, their extra-biblical revelation is given greater authority and importance than the Bible.

It is interesting to note that most cult leaders who have received "new revelations" have acknowledged receiving them during encounters with spirit beings. A look behind the scenes will reveal a definite association with the occult and contact with demonic beings that masquerade as angelic beings, spirits of the dead, or even Christ Himself.

Now realize, a cult leader who is attempting to gain followers for his "new revelation" is usually not so naive as to immediately attempt to persuade "Christians" to accept his/her "extreme" ideas and beliefs. Instead, they will give some general truths that almost everyone agrees with and talk about God, Christ, the Bible, miracles, etc. The immature and unsuspecting listener is impressed. Very subtly the cultist reveals his "new revelation" of false doctrine mixed with just enough truth to keep you off-guard. Finally the cultist reveals that his true allegiance is to some book or teaching other than the Bible and someone other than Jesus Christ.

Cultists are usually successful in proclaiming their "new truth" to those who have little of the "old truth." But in reality their message is not new at all. Ecclesiastes 1:9, 10 states, "...there is nothing new under the sun. Is there anything of which one might say, 'See this, it is new'? Already it has existed for ages which were before us."

So although they claim to have God's "new revelation"

for the world, it is really just new names and disguises for Satan's old methods of leading people away from the God of the Bible and from His revealed truth in Jesus Christ.

At a time when thousands of New Age messiahs and prophets are attempting to gain followers for their "new revelations," Galatians 1:8 warns, "But even though we, or an angel from heaven, should preach to you a gospel contrary to that which we have preached to you, let him be accursed."[12]

Evaluate All Things in the Light of Scripture

When problems concerning issues and new teachings arose in the early New Testament Church, believers evaluated them in light of Old Testament Scripture. For example, in Acts 15:13–19, James uses Old Testament Scripture to provide the Apostles' conclusion regarding the Gospel being proclaimed to the Gentiles.

So too, in these last days, we must evaluate all so-called prophecies and "new revelations" in light of Scripture. When they run contrary to Scripture, no matter how good they sound, no matter how anointed they seem, we must reject them. If we don't, we will soon be following "another Jesus," not the actual Jesus of the Bible; "another spirit," not the true Holy Spirit; and "another gospel," not the genuine biblical Gospel (2 Corinthians 11:4).

In a personal letter my wife received from David Wilkerson, he wrote, "Personally, I never stray from the Word and I do not give much credence to much of what is called personal prophecy and new revelation. Ninety-nine percent of it is zeal without wisdom, repetitious, and absolutely nothing new except error. We are safest when we stay rock solid on the Word."

There is a Need for Biblical Balance

1 Corinthians 14:29–33 admonishes: "Let the prophets speak two or three, and let the other judge. If any thing be revealed to another that sitteth by, let the first hold his peace. For ye may all prophesy one by one, that all may learn, and all may be comforted. And the spirits of the prophets are subject to the prophets. For God is not the author of confusion, but of peace, as in all churches of the saints."

1 Thessalonians 5:19–21 gives us what I believe to be one of the most balanced Scriptures on prophecy. It states: "Quench not the Spirit. Despise not prophesyings. Prove all things; hold fast that which is good."

We have an obligation to allow the manifestation of the gifts of the Spirit, but a responsibility to evaluate everything in light of Scripture. We should hold fast to that which is good, but reject what is not in accord with God's Word.

In contradiction of the above verses, many self-proclaimed and man-appointed prophets think they are above questioning and refuse to be evaluated. They twist Scripture, manipulate followers, and make alignments with pastors and "prophets" to avoid being biblically critiqued.

These supposed modern-day prophets and apostles hinder their followers from being like the noble Bereans who not only received the word with great eagerness but also examined the Scriptures daily to see whether these things were so (Acts 17:11). As a result, there is rampant false teaching under the guise of prophecies and new revelations.

Although Jesus rebuked the church of Ephesus for leaving its first love, He commended it for not tolerating evil men and putting to the test those who called themselves apostles, and were not, but were found to be false (Revelation 2:2).

I Believe in Prophecy

I believe the gift of prophecy is for today. The Church needs to be encouraged, corrected, and built up with messages from the heart of God—delivered in the power of His Spirit and by inspiration of His Word.

Genuine prophetic utterances will always be in harmony with God's written revelation, the Holy Scriptures. Prophecy is not merely foretelling future events, but often *forth-telling* the mind and will of God.

Revelation 19:10 states, "And I fell at his feet to worship him. And he said unto me, See thou do it not: I am thy fellowservant, and of thy brethren that have the testimony of Jesus: worship God: for the testimony of Jesus is the spirit of prophecy."

Concerning true prophecy in the Church, Scripture states: "But if all prophesy, and there come in one that believeth not, or one unlearned, he is convinced of all, he is judged of all: And thus are the secrets of his heart made manifest; and so falling down on his face he will worship God, and report that God is in you of a truth" (1 Corinthians14: 24, 25).

The sad reality is that much of what goes on in Christian circles today is not the genuine gift of prophecy. Instead of pro-claiming the true word of the Lord under the anointing of the Holy Spirit, we are often given a poor imitation, prophesying from one's own inspiration, or a demonic counterfeit.

Instead of "Christianized fortune-telling" the body of Christ needs those who have truly heard from the Lord and are accurately proclaiming, "Thus saith the Lord."

I admonish you not to accept as genuine a prophecy or revelation from anyone, unless it is in exact accord with God's Word, is 100 percent accurate (or has the potential future fulfillment of being 100% accurate), confirms what His Spirit has already spoken to your heart, truly exalts the Jesus of the Bible, and draws you closer to Him.

Never accept prophecies and revelations as higher authority than Scripture or make anyone, except Jesus Christ, the director of your life. Do not run to others for quick prophetic advice but seek guidance from God's Word. Be sensitive and yielded so His Spirit can speak to your heart. Spend time in prayer and fasting as you wait upon the Lord. Be led by His Spirit. And always honor Him and obey His Word.

Chapter Six

SHOULD OUR EXPERIENCE GO BEYOND GOD'S WORD?

Jim Weikal has been a friend and colleague for many years, serving as Biblical Instruction Director at my ministry for over a decade and now pastor of a church. He has a strong commitment to know and defend biblical Christianity. This chapter, therefore, was written by Jim, at my request.

An eagerness to see the Holy Spirit manifest in a mighty way has led to a faulty method of evaluation—personal experience, feelings, and emotion. As a result, multitudes of people are embracing unbiblical beliefs, practices, and phenomena.

To discern properly whether a supernatural move is from God or the adversary, we must apply the Scriptures.

"Study to shew thyself approved unto God, a workman that needeth not to be ashamed, rightly dividing the word of truth" (2 Timothy 2:15).

To correctly handle the Word of truth requires years of hard work—time, study, memorization, commitment, discipline, vigilance, and the like. It is written: "All scripture is given by inspiration of God, and is profitable for doctrine, for reproof, for correction, for instruction in righteousness" (2 Timothy 3:16).

The Bible is clear on the issue of faith and practice. More than seventy times the phrases "it is written" or "according to the Word" are used when the author wishes to show authority for his position.

Why do people insist on calling Jesus "Lord, Lord" and then not do what He says? Why do people say they diligently study the Scriptures and love the Lord, but when the Scriptures show no validation for much of today's spiritual phenomena, proponents say, "This is a new move of the Spirit that goes beyond the Word of God"? They ignore the lack of biblical support.

The idea that adherence to the Word of God would offend the Holy Spirit, and therefore quench Him, is human speculation and incorrect. Extreme groups, liberal theologians, ecumenical organizations, and the like disdain the notion of biblical authority because it destroys their distorted views and spirit of compromise. Encouraging people to ignore the teachings of Scripture , they embrace "a new move of God."

When Jesus came into the world, He did not ask the Jews if they felt He was the Messiah. He used references to prophecy: "And he said unto them, These are the words which I spake unto you, while I was yet with you, that all things must be fulfilled, which were written in the law of Moses, and in the prophets, and in the psalms, concerning me" (Luke 24:44).

He expected those listening to Him to search the Scriptures. Why should we do any differently? Has the body of Christ totally forgotten Paul's warning about the last days? "Let no man deceive you by any means: for that day shall not come, except there come a falling away first, and that man of sin be revealed, the son of perdition" (2 Thessalonians 2:3).

There is an apostasy from the faith "which was once delivered to the saints" (Jude 3). Jesus asked in Luke 18:8, "When the Son of man cometh, shall he find faith on the earth?"

Jesus was speaking of faith in Him. Unfortunately, many will answer, "Yes." But their faith will be in false christs, false prophets, false signs, false wonders, and false miracles!

Is the body of Christ so deficient in biblical discernment that any supernatural experience can be perceived as coming from God simply because leaders say it is, or the experience feels so good it has to be from God?

We are given in the book of Acts, chapters 2 and 4, an account of the greatest revival in New Testament times, where the three thousand and five thousand were added to the church. In neither of these instances is there information given of any unusual happenings by the converts themselves.

To come against the Holy Spirit is dangerous, and I don't know of any true Christian who wants to knowingly do that. But, on the other hand, I don't know of any Christian who knowingly wants to embrace a false or demonic spirit. To know the difference we must have the authority contained in the Bible.

When advocating that Scripture is the standard for evaluating spiritual matters and not experience or feelings, many biblical references can be found:

1. a) "Why do thy disciples transgress the tradition of the elders? for they wash not their hands when they eat bread. But he answered and said unto them, Why do ye also transgress the commandment of God by your tradition?" (Matthew 15:2, 3).

b) He was also saying to them, "Full well ye reject the commandment of God, that ye may keep your own tradition" (Mark 7:9).

To evaluate Scripture based simply on what tradition says or on some experience of the past is dangerous. Just because something occurred in the past does not automatically make it right. To refer back to revivals and say, "Well it happened then, so it must be okay now," is using a faulty method of getting at the truth. For if what was done then was wrong, it is just as wrong now. Don't set aside Scripture for the sake of sensations.

2. "And when they shall say unto you, Seek unto them that have familiar spirits, and unto wizards that peep, and that mutter: should not a people seek unto their God? for the living to the dead? To the law and to the testimony: if they speak not according to this word, it is because there is no light in them" (Isaiah 8:19, 20).

Even in the time of the prophet Isaiah, the law and the testimony were the standards for judging belief and practice.

3. "But have renounced the hidden things of dishonesty, not walking in craftiness, nor handling the word of God deceitfully; but by manifestation of the truth commending ourselves to every man's conscience in the sight of God" (2 Corinthians 4:2).

The Word of God should not have to be distorted or twisted to advance some belief or practice. Let the truth of God's Word speak to the issue and judge accordingly.

4. "For I testify unto every man that heareth the words of the prophecy of this book, If any man shall add unto these things, God shall add unto him the plagues that are written in this book; And if any man shall take away from the words of the book of this prophecy, God shall take away his part out of the book of life, and out of the holy city, and from the things which are written in this book" (Revelation 22:18, 19).

People who are saying that God is doing a new move (which goes beyond His Word) are standing on dangerous ground.

5. "The LORD thy God will raise up unto thee a Prophet from the midst of thee, of thy brethren, like unto me; unto him ye shall hearken; According to all that thou desiredst of the LORD thy God in Horeb in the day of the assembly, saying, Let me not hear again the voice of the LORD my God, neither let me see this great fire any more, that I die not. And the LORD said unto me, They have well spoken that which they have spoken. I will raise them up a Prophet from among their brethren, like unto thee, and will put my words in his mouth; and he shall speak unto them all that I shall command him. And it shall come to pass, that whosoever will not hearken unto my words which he shall speak in my name, I will require it of him" (Deuteronomy 18:15–19).

Notice in the next verse that Jesus rebuked the Jews for not believing what had been written about Him: For had ye believed Moses, ye would have believed me; for he wrote of me (John 5:46).

6. These next two verses point to the same concept—
    understand what the Scriptures say and act according to
    their teachings:

"In the last day, that great day of the feast, Jesus stood
and cried, saying, If any man thirst, let him come unto
me, and drink. He that believeth on me, as the scripture
hath said, out of his belly shall flow rivers of living water"
(John 7:37, 38).

"Many of the people therefore, when they heard this saying, said, Of a truth this is the Prophet" (John 7:40).

7. This is that Moses, which said unto the children of
    Israel, A prophet shall the Lord your God raise up unto
    you of your brethren, like unto me; him shall ye hear"
    (Acts 7:37).

Stephen used the Scriptures to prove his beliefs just before he
was martyred (Acts 7).

8. And after the reading of the law and the prophets the
    rulers of the synagogue sent unto them, saying, Ye men
    and brethren, if ye have any word of exhortation for the
    people, say on" (Acts 13:15).

Continuing in verse 16 of Acts chapter 13, Paul addresses the
Jews at Antioch about Jesus Christ. Paul begins by relating historical facts from the Scriptures the Jews knew so well—the stay
in Egypt, the wandering in the desert, the period of the judges
and the kings, and the promise of a Savior. When Paul gets to

the preaching of John the Baptist and Jesus' life, death, and resurrection, he shows how Scripture has been fulfilled by quoting from the Psalms and the Prophets. Paul used historical facts and Scriptural truth to authenticate his reasoning.

We need to understand that any line of reasoning takes us down some path. If our reasoning begins with man's experience and emotion as the basis for determining God's truth, that path will lead to apostasy. Emotion and experience are important to the spiritual life, and God wants worshippers with passion and feeling toward Him. But without a biblical starting point and Scriptural "guardrails" on both sides, the believer is headed down a meandering, hazard-filled path paved with confusion, delusion, and doctrinal error.

Consider the following passages: "And Paul, as his manner was, went in unto them, and three sabbath days reasoned with them out of the scriptures, Opening and alleging, that Christ must needs have suffered, and risen again from the dead; and that this Jesus, whom I preach unto you, is Christ. And some of them believed, and consorted with Paul and Silas; and of the devout Greeks a great multitude, and of the chief women not a few" (Acts 17:2–4).

> "And the brethren immediately sent away Paul and Silas by night unto Berea: who coming thither went into the synagogue of the Jews. These were more noble than those in Thessalonica, in that they received the word with all readiness of mind, and searched the scriptures daily, whether those things were so" (Acts 17:10, 11).

The message of Jesus, Stephen, Paul, and other leaders of the early church is loud and clear: The Scriptures are the final authority in spiritual affairs—not feelings, emotions, intuition, past revivals, personal testimonies, prophecies, movements, or the enthusiastic crowd.

I want to thank Jim Weikal for contributing this timely and significant chapter. As Christians seeking a biblical lifestyle, God's Word must remain central to our experience.

Chapter Seven

FALSE SIGNS AND MIRACLES

Holy Laughter, Being Drunk In the Spirit...

Just like in the days of Jesus (Luke 11:29), today's generation wants to see signs and wonders. As a result, they will follow almost any spiritual leader who promises the "miraculous."

Now there is nothing wrong with feelings, emotions, and excitement, for these can be valid responses to the genuine moving of the Holy Spirit. Moreover, we are not to quench the Spirit who desires to work in our lives in a real and special way. The danger arises when people begin seeking experiences, miracles, signs, and revelations more than they seek the Lord and His Word.

I certainly realize that many churches could sure use a little more excitement and enthusiasm. Some are so dead and cold that you feel as if you are at a funeral home. Other churches have gone to the opposite extreme and focus on sensationalism and emotionalism, manifesting little discernment and knowledge of God's Word. They have replaced the message of the Gospel with a "show." In too many cases the church is becoming a center for entertainment and mysticism.

Somewhere between the boring, loveless, and lifeless church, and the church that specializes in the spectacular and the supernatural, is the biblically-balanced church. We need to allow God's Spirit to move in a dynamic and exciting way. But we must remember, the same Apostle Paul who demonstrated the thrilling power of the resurrected Christ, as he evangelized new frontiers and wrote much of the New Testament, also warned against false teachers, counterfeit miracles, and the misuse of the gifts of the Holy Spirit.

I Believe in the Gifts of the Spirit

After I spoke at a Full Gospel banquet, a woman came up to me and said, "You are so refreshing to hear because I see so much error and deception today. It is exciting to see someone like you who believes in the gifts of the Spirit, but who is also warning about the counterfeit and the fakery going on. We need to have that kind of balance and credibility."

I believe in the gifts of the Spirit. I have seen genuine healings and miracles through faith in Christ. In fact, in an upcoming book entitled, *The Impossible,* I am documenting some of the miraculous interventions the Lord has done in my life and ministry.

I have seen the genuine power and moving of God's Spirit. I have also seen the imitation of flesh, and the demonic counterfeit. Experience-oriented people who lack discernment and who allow phenomena to determine their beliefs, instead of evaluating and lining up their experiences with the Word of God, are easy prey for exploitation and counterfeit experiences, which they accept as genuinely from God.

Purpose of the Spirit

One of the main purposes of the Holy Spirit is to empower God's people to boldly and effectively witness for the truth of Jesus Christ (Acts 1:8; John 15:26). The gifts of the Spirit are to exalt Jesus and draw people to Him—not draw attention to the person operating the gift. Miracles have been used by God to validate His messengers (2 Corinthians 12:12) and confirm the truth of the message being proclaimed. Acts 14:3 says: "Long time therefore abode they speaking boldly in the Lord, which gave testimony unto the word of his grace, and granted signs and wonders to be done by their hands."

The gifts of the Holy Spirit are also to exhort and strengthen the body of Christ—but not so believers can merely have a "good time" enjoying exotic, bizarre, and often, useless displays of extraordinary feats and phenomena. More than signs and wonders, my heart's desire is for the Holy Spirit's presence in power to bring deep conviction (1 Thessalonians 1:5) on the hearts of those hearing the proclamation of God's Word. I want to be used to turn the hearts of the people to the Lord and to motivate them to walk in faithfulness until He returns.

The Holy Spirit convicts (exposes and convinces) the world concerning sin, righteousness, and judgment (John 16:8). *The Full Life Study Bible* footnote on this matter states: "Through the manifestation of the Spirit among God's people, sin will be exposed, repentance called for, and sinners convicted. Where there is no exposing of unrighteousness, no conviction of sin or no plea for repentance, the Holy Spirit is clearly not at work according to the biblical pattern."[13]

Most Are a Poor Imitation or Counterfeit

When I read in Scripture the message Paul, Peter, and John proclaimed, it is far different from much of what is being heard today. And most "miracles" today don't resemble at all the miracles God performed in the early Church as recorded in Acts.

From research, studying God's Word, and knowing His voice through prayer and fasting, I must conclude that much of what is being passed off today as the Holy Spirit is a poor imitation. It more resembles an energy force or spirit guide than the Holy Spirit of the Bible.

While some churches are experiencing a genuine move of God's Spirit, much of what I see as I travel throughout the world is imitation and counterfeit. It is emotionalism, hype, the power of suggestion, psychological manipulation, mass hysteria, and psychosomatic manifestations. Some of it is outright fakery, or worse yet, a demonic counterfeit.

Even though I have seen the Lord do some incredible things, the Church today has not yet witnessed the full outpouring of His Spirit as described in the book of Acts and in the prophecies of the second chapter of Joel. However, I believe an authentic outpouring of God's Spirit is on the near horizon—before His Second Coming.

God is about to pour out His Spirit in a powerful way on believers who maintain a testimony for the Jesus of the Bible, remain faithful to His Word, and who have spiritual discernment, thereby, refusing the imitation and counterfeit.

Leaders "Perform" to Keep Excitement

One of the reasons for so much nonsense in many churches is because those in leadership do not have the genuine moving of God's Spirit, but feel tremendous pressure to "perform" to keep the church growing and excited. As a result, many pastors and leaders resort to gimmicks, emotionalism, and even New Age techniques to generate excitement to keep followers coming.

Phillip Keller writes concerning much of these phenomena in his book, *Predators In Our Pulpits:*

> The main objective is simply to satisfy the crowds. Their demand for an exciting experience...must be met. The end result is that millions of earnest, seeking souls have been given a bowl full of sensationalism but scarcely a crumb of truth. They come with searching spirits that can only be truly satisfied by the presence of the Living Christ. They go away deceived into believing that they have been touched by God's Spirit when in fact it was largely a sham and show...
>
> An even more serious dimension of their spiritual deception lies in the fact that they are often led to believe a lie. Exciting revelations, stimulating prophecies, erotic encounters (often counterfeited by false teaching), and spurious spirits lead the gullible ones...[14]

Usurping the Place of the Holy Spirit

Christian leaders who in any way attempt to "create" spiritual experiences for their followers must realize they are not helping God, they are usurping the place of the Holy Spirit and undermining the Gospel. They are powerless and they know it, so they turn to these other techniques in an attempt to impress people. But I have traveled in too many Christian circles and have seen too many things, both in front of and behind the scenes, to be gullible and influenced by these kinds of inferior phenomena.

Satan is deceiving many Christians into accepting a pseudo spiritual experience so they will be desensitized to not truly seek the Lord or the genuine outpouring of His Spirit. All the hoopla camouflages the lack of real Holy Spirit manifestations. The *external* displays act as a smoke screen to conceal the lack of *internal* commitment to the true Jesus of Scripture.

It Mirrored the Shallow, Wild Times of the World

As a brand-new Christian at the age of eighteen I got caught up in a group of some supposed super-spiritual Christians, which specialized in all the signs and wonders. So-called supernatural phenomena such as healings, miracles, being slain in the Spirit, laughing and dancing in the Spirit, revelations, personal prophecies, angelic encounters, visions, casting demons out of Christians, and vomiting up demons were the norm.

Having just given up my former wild lifestyle in the world, it was most appealing to discover (or so I thought) that I could replace it with a wild lifestyle of continual miracles and the supernatural. But I soon discovered that most of the people in this group were too busy chasing the excitement and the signs and wonders to have time to seek the Lord through prayer and fasting and diligently studying His Word. As a result, they lacked the necessary spiritual discernment and Scripture knowledge to realize they were into beliefs and practices that were contrary to God's Word and definitely not of His Spirit.

Besides, their walk with the Lord was like a yo-yo. When the supposed miracles and ecstatic experiences were happening to them, they praised and served the Lord, but when they were not, they quickly fell away. Today, almost all this group is far away from the Lord because they built their walk on emotions, excitement, and the sensational, rather than the Scriptural principles of commitment, obedience, and discipline.

I quickly realized that just as the wild parties and getting high before accepting Christ were only short-lived pleasures, so too, this hyper-emotional lifestyle did not bring the long-lasting spiritual fulfillment I desired. The only way to be totally fulfilled spiritually is to desire the Lord with all your heart, walk in fellowship with Him, and be obedient to His Word and Spirit. As a result, I would soon witness His miraculous power, but not the carnival atmosphere of before. And it would not be by my initiation or manipulation, but by His sovereign intervention.

As I reflect back on the highlights of my life and ministry, I am aware of the many miracles the Lord has done. By focusing on these miracles out of context with the rest of my life, it might seem as though I experienced constant miracles. However, sometimes I went for months or even more than a year through a wilderness where God molded and trained me without any apparent supernatural intervention. In the same way, if you take Scripture out of context when looking at the lives of Daniel, Moses, Elijah, Paul, and others, it may seem like they had constant miracles. The total picture, however, shows this not to be true.

Psychosomatic Healings

To maintain integrity in the body of Christ, I must also say that many claiming to have a healing ministry are merely doing psychosomatic healings—not genuine divine healing.

A world-famous evangelist spoke for over two hours yet quoted only a few Scriptures. The rest of the time he talked about his experiences and his vision from the Lord.

The affirmative statements he had everyone repeat as a confession of being blessed were almost like chanting, and many in the audience seemed to be in an altered state of consciousness—almost a trance-like state—as they repeated them.

During the altar call he had those who came forward raise both of their hands high in the air. Then he would hit them on their foreheads. Some wobbled and a few fell down.

There were also some supposed healings, but they were merely psychosomatic. The two that were in wheelchairs left unchanged, as did all the others who had visible afflictions.

I heard another popular evangelist who frequently bragged about his healing ministry. At a national convention I attended, there were many supposed healings, but once again they were psychosomatic. A woman who was brought in on an ambulance cot and others with obvious medical conditions left the same way they came.

Blatantly False Healings

The national secretary of a well-respected movement in India with over two thousand churches told me that he never saw one genuine healing in India by all the so-called popular healing evangelists that came through. He told me that an American evangelist had a large healing crusade in India. Thousands of dollars were spent on posters, advertising, and feeding people after the services to draw big crowds. He was aware of several people in India who were paid to come and fake healings and then testify how they were healed.

The evangelist told people to raise one hand if they had any prayer requests. At that very moment his staff took photographs to bring back to the U.S. claiming these people were in the process of giving their lives to Jesus. Then he would ask them to raise both hands, photograph them with their hands in the air, and claim to his supporters that these people were praising the Lord.

The national secretary said to me, "A militant Hindu group brought ten blind and crippled people and told this evangelist they would give ten thousand U.S. dollars if he healed just one of them, but the evangelist would not even pray for them." (Why didn't he tell them to keep their money, but he would still pray?)

The national secretary said he saw no lasting fruit from these pseudo-miracle crusades. All the people wanted was the excitement—very few wanted true salvation.

Many people are becoming hostile to the Gospel because of the fakery they see in Jesus' name. If we are going to win a skeptical world to Christ we must do so with integrity and the true anointing of His Spirit.

At a crusade in Nigeria, an apostle over several churches prayed loud and emotionally with those who came forward. He pushed on their heads and most of them fell over backwards, supposedly falling under the power of God. But it was soon proven to be all emotion and hype. Right after a teenage girl was "slain in the Spirit," a ten-year-old blind girl with no eyes in her sockets was brought up for prayer for a healing. After this apostle yelled and hollered and pushed on her head, guess what happened? Nothing! She left the same way she came.

The same Spirit, which had allegedly knocked down all those people, surely could have restored this girl's eyesight. But God's Spirit was not moving. It was merely hype and emotion.

I have witnessed this happen over and over. Sure, there are many claims of healings—but either the claims were not verifiable, or the healings were merely psychosomatic. I have yet to discover even one legitimate healing of the caliber of Jesus, Paul, Peter to be accomplished by faith healers who resort to unbiblical phenomena and techniques. In fact, the ones operating this supposed gift from God almost always avoid the people who obviously need a real supernatural touch from the Lord if they are going to *truly* be healed.

However, the time is coming when God is going to pour out His Spirit and amazing healings and miracles will occur. But Scripture also prophesies that false prophets and false messiahs are going to perform great signs and counterfeit miracles (Matthew 24:24). So once again, the only way to know what is of God, the flesh, or the devil, will be to have discernment from studying God's Word and spending time in prayer and fasting.

Compare Today's Show with Our Lord's Example

While imitators perform "miracles" to impress people, Jesus did miracles out of compassion and to the glory of God. His miracles were a sign and validation of His message and Messianic claims. Jesus and the apostles did not go around merely healing invisible ailments such as headaches, joint pain, and so on. They healed visible organic maladies and injuries—blind eyes, withered hands, crippled limbs, paralysis, leprosy, a severed ear, and the like. They even raised the dead. Those healed in Scripture did not have to confess, claim, or visualize for days or weeks their healing before it occurred. The healings of Jesus were usually immediate, complete, irreversible, and undeniable even to His opponents and critics.

When we think of the "miracles" performed by today's faith healers, could we honestly say what Nicodemus said to Jesus: "The same came to Jesus by night, and said unto him, Rabbi, we know that thou art a teacher come from God: for no man can do these miracles that thou doest, except God be with him" (John 3:2).

Or how about Paul in Lystra, when God used him to heal a man "impotent in his feet, being a cripple from his mother's womb, who never had walked" (Acts 14:8). The crowds were so impressed with Paul's undeniable miracle that they said, "The gods are come down to us in the likeness of men" (Acts 14:11). You can read more about this amazing account and what led to Paul's stoning and apparent resurrection in Acts chapter 14.

Those whom God is really using today in supernatural healings do very little boasting about it. You will not find them advertising their gift in Christian magazines or on radio, television, or the Internet. They are serving the Lord in places and ways through which they will probably not get much worldly credit. But one day they will receive the Lord's reward for their faithfulness and for allowing His power to be manifested through their lives—without attempting to use it to exalt themselves, advance their own ministries, or obtain financial gain.

Prayer Cloths and Handkerchiefs

Dr. B.J. Rudge shares some helpful insights in this section on prayer cloths and handkerchiefs.

In Acts 19:11, 12 we read that God performed "special miracles by the hands of Paul" to the extent that even Paul's handkerchiefs and aprons were used to heal people. Unfortunately, many have mis-applied this passage. The following are a few thoughts to consider.

First: The extraordinary way in which God worked through Paul was relevant to the audience that Paul was directing his missionary efforts. Ephesus was a city known for its magic arts and supernatural occurrences. God's Spirit performed miracles through Paul that demonstrated Jesus' power over demonic pow-ers. In contrast, in cities like Athens, where the orientation was to the philosophical, there are no miracles reported, but Paul's presentation of the Gospel was tailored to the speculative bent of his listeners. This may provide us with our principle. The Gospel confronts human beings where they are spiritually. Where there is demonism and sorcery, the Holy Spirit may act to demonstrate the lordship of Jesus. Where there is moral and mental darkness, the Spirit may act through the holy lives of God's people and the simple message of the Gospel to demonstrate that in Jesus there is a better way. This point highlights once again that the miraculous events of Acts 19:11, 12 were specifically performed by Paul for the people of Ephesus. Since the Ephesians lived in a city known for its magic arts and sorcery, God empowered Paul to perform miraculous acts in Ephesus that would demonstrate the lordship of Jesus Christ.

Second: These miracles performed by Paul are not normative (standard for how God normally works) but are unique (or as Luke says in Acts "extraordinary") acts by God, specific to the situation found in Acts chapter 19. The Greek word *tuchon* (extraordinary) can be better translated "not common" or "special." Throughout the New Testament, we find only two other instances of similar miracles: Peter's shadow (Acts 5:15) and Jesus' garment (Mark 5:27–34; 6:56). Also, realize that Paul goes to numerous cities where there is no record of him performing any miracles (Pisidian Antioch, Athens, Berea, Corinth, and Thessalonica). This should show us that the events of Acts 19 are unique/special/not common in nature.

Third: It should be noted that God performed these miracles only through Paul. Nowhere in the book of Acts do we see God working these specific miracles through other believers in the same way that He did through Paul in Ephesus. This should not be surprising since Paul was God's chosen instrument to preach the Gospel to the Gentiles (Acts 9:15). Paul was empowered in unique and extraordinary ways to demonstrate that his authority came from God Almighty. One should be extremely cautious of attributing to himself/herself "extraordinary" events that God chose to do through the Apostle Paul.

Fourth: The main purpose of these miracles was to authenticate or confirm the message of the apostle Paul. As we continue to read chapter 19, we see that many people came to accept Jesus Christ as their Lord and Savior as they turned from their former way of living (vss. 18–20). These miracles demonstrated to the Ephesians the power and truth of the Gospel of Jesus Christ, which in turn would bring them to repentance. The miracles were never intended to draw people to Paul. Rather, they were used to point the Ephesians to Jesus Christ, who alone deserves all glory, honor, and praise.

Although Acts 19:12 cannot be used to support the use and sale of "prayer cloths and handkerchiefs," one can be assured that God does work today through supernatural means. He uses healings and miracles to demonstrate the truth of the Gospel message. When God does choose to perform extraordinary miracles today, we would expect at least the following to be present:

1) These miracles would point people exclusively to Jesus Christ.
2) These miracles would most likely occur in an area, like ancient Ephesus, which was dominated by the occult and magic.
3) These miracles would lead to a true spiritual revival where we would see people repenting of their evil ways and turning to faith in Christ, as happened in Ephesus (Acts 19:18–20).

The church today has lost true spiritual power as it seeks after cheap imitations. Therefore, believers need to get back to the basic principles that made the early church in the book of Acts a powerful witness for Jesus Christ (see Acts 2:42, 43). By devoting oneself to the study of God's word, pursuing a life of prayer, and walking in the Spirit, perhaps the church today, as in the book of Acts, will see the authentic display of God's miraculous power.

"Slain in the Spirit"

As a new Christian I was very open to being "slain in the Spirit," but I was not the type who would be pushed down or fall on my own. Many who had this phenomenon manifest in their ministries would lay hands on me, expecting the power of God to knock me down. Some had me close my eyes and raise my hands and then pushed hard against my forehead, but I never went down. Those who endorse this phenomenon might say, "Well, you did not go down because you resisted." But that is not true; I was very

NOT OUR FATHER'S FAITH

open to it. I am just not easily influenced or manipulated by such emotionalism and phenomena.

If it really were the power of God's Spirit which had "slain" these people, then He could also drop them unhurt to the ground without the need for catchers. And they should get up off the floor being genuinely healed or delivered.

David Wilkerson said it well: "If people are going to fall down, I want to see them falling under the conviction of the Holy Ghost. And the vision I want them to receive is a renewed vision of Jesus. And the manifestation I want them to have is their rising from the floor as a new creature in Christ!"[15]

In Scripture, believers fell on their faces in awe and worship before the Lord (Abraham—Genesis 17:1–3; Joshua 5:13–15; Ezekiel 1:28; 3:23; 43:1–5; 44:4; Daniel 8:15–18, 27; 10:7–11; disciples at transfiguration—Matthew 17:5,6; angels and elders—Revelation 7:11; 11:16, 17). And the experience happened directly between God and the individual—no human being had to lay hands on them, and none fell after being lined up and blown on.

Even the book that deals extensively with end-time prophecy (Revelation) nowhere states anything about being "slain in the Spirit." Even when one was in the very presence of God, there is no such phenomenon mentioned. But there are several accounts in Revelation of His people who by their own volition fall on their faces to worship Him in awe and reverence (Revelation 4:9, 10; 7:11; 11:16).

Stand Up on Your Feet

Those who experience being "slain in the Spirit" usually fall backward, which contradicts all biblical accounts for believers. Only in such cases as when Jesus said "I am He" to the unbelieving soldiers who were arresting Him did they draw back and fall to the ground.

The Scriptural accounts which proponents use to endorse "slain in the Spirit" are taken out of context. Besides, Scriptural records indicate that the Lord often tells those overwhelmed by His presence and fall on their faces to get up so He can speak to them—not lay there for several minutes to several hours doing "carpet time" while the Lord supposedly speaks and ministers to them. The following examples of Scripture bear this out:

Ezekiel 1:28, 2:2: "As the appearance of the bow that is in the cloud in the day of rain, so was the appearance of the brightness round about. This was the appearance of the likeness of the glory of the LORD. And when I saw it, I fell upon my face, and I heard a voice of one that spake. And the spirit entered into me when he spake unto me, and set me upon my feet, that I heard him that spake unto me."

Ezekiel 3:23, 24: "Then I arose, and went forth into the plain: and, behold, the glory of the LORD stood there, as the glory which I saw by the river of Chebar: and I fell on my face. Then the spirit entered into me, and set me upon my feet…"

Matthew 17:6, 7: "And when the disciples heard it, they fell on their face, and were sore afraid. And Jesus came and touched them, and said, Arise, and be not afraid."

(Also see Ezekiel 43:1–5; Daniel 8:15–18; 10:7–11; and Acts 9:3–8.)

There is no record in Scripture of believers "falling under the power of the Spirit" when Jesus or the apostles laid hands on them and prayed for them. Yet in many circles people line up to have hands laid on them in order to receive this euphoric experience.

I have seen many people "slain in the Spirit"—some even

at churches while I was ministering or praying for them, but it was not my doing or the Spirit's. I am not saying their hearts or motives were impure, but the reasons for its occurrence are many and varied including predetermining before the meeting they would be "slain," equilibrium problem, loss of balance due to eyes being closed and hands raised, power of suggestion, being conditioned and programmed, mind control, mass hypnosis, and even sometimes demonic manifestation (the possession-trance-state of shamanism).

It is obvious from extensive research, the associated other phenomena and teachings that often occur along with it, and evaluating Scripture in context, being "slain in the Spirit" is not Scriptural.

Most can only give their experience as proof that it is from God. However, when proponents venture to give Scripture to validate being "slain in the Spirit," once they are examined in context, it is clearly evident that what is happening today is as far removed from the biblical accounts as a backyard carnival is from Disneyland.

"Close Encounters" in Toronto

A missionary couple I met while ministering in Haiti had attended a church in Toronto when the "holy laughter" first began to mani-fest. They told me they were greatly confused by this unscriptural phenomenon, but were unable to voice their opinion lest they be considered unspiritual. When I asked them if they felt what was going on there was of God, the flesh, or demonic, they quickly replied, "Much of it was demonic."

A team of us (some who were raised in and attend Pentecostal and Charismatic churches) visited the Toronto church and by then it had progressed beyond uncontrollable laughter and weeping, to people being "drunk in the Spirit," struck dumb, and stuck like glue. We witnessed people doing every imaginable contortion, twitching, and jerking movement. Many of them fell backwards in ecstatic trances or their bodies shook violently out of control. While the speaker was trying to preach, we heard gut-wrenching groans, shrieks, warrior cries, animal noises, and a garbled "prophecy" by a pastor's wife who acted like a wild woman shaking, jerking, and swirling her head around in quick spasmodic motions. Parts of the service resembled a voodoo ritual, people on drugs, or a psychiatric ward, more than a Spirit-filled service. To think that tens of thousands of people and pastors had visited this place…many to take the "blessing" back to their churches.

When I returned from Toronto, my Bible study just happened to appropriately include 2 Timothy 4:1–5 which says: "I charge thee therefore before God, and the Lord Jesus Christ, who shall judge the quick and the dead at his appearing and his kingdom; Preach the word; be instant in season, out of season; reprove, rebuke, exhort with all long suffering and doctrine. For the time will come when they will not endure sound doctrine; but after their own lusts shall they heap to themselves teachers, having itching ears; And they shall turn away their ears from the truth, and shall be turned unto fables. But watch thou in all things…"

"Holy Laughter"

Just as there is no real Scriptural support for being "slain in the Spirit," there is no Scriptural basis for the phenomenon called "holy laughter."

I am all for "the joy of the Lord" (Nehemiah 8:10), and am well aware that "a joyful heart is good medicine" (Proverbs 17:22). There is nothing wrong with laughing and being joyful. "Holy laughter," however, is a diabolical deception.

"Holy Ghost bartenders" served the "new wine" of "holy laughter" and encouraged people to "belly-on-up to the bar." Adherents were told to surrender to the laughter (I thought we should only surrender to the Lord) and just "let go."

People fell on the floor and convulsed in uncontrollable laughter or giggling—sometimes for hours. Some laughed hysterically while others cried. Some rolled around on the floor. Some danced "sensually" while some men fell and laid on women or women on men. Others had out-of-body experiences and claimed to have seen visions or angels. I also saw participants (many being pastors) jerking, shaking violently, roaring like lions, barking like dogs, and hissing and writhing like snakes—definite occult phenomena. Hours later, some staggered out of the church or laughed uncontrollably while driving down the road or eating at restaurants.

This bizarre phenomena was fed by a major misconception and twisting of Scripture—that being filled with the Spirit produces the same effect on a person as being drunk on wine.

The irrational behavior described above has absolutely no Scriptural basis. In fact, Ephesians 5:18, one of the passages used most often in support of this kind of experience, actually means the exact opposite of what is being propagated.

Immature and biblically illiterate Christians have been erroneously led to believe that because this text says that Christians should not get drunk on wine, but should be filled with the Spirit, that it means "don't get drunk on wine, get drunk on the Spirit." However, based on research done as part of an exegetical study in the original Greek language on Ephesians 5:18 and 19, David Sabella concludes:

> When the verse is examined within its Scriptural context and with an understanding of the historical and cultural background into which it was written, it is obvious that Paul is here calling for sobriety and *not* intoxication of any kind. He is commanding the Church not to worship as the hellenistic cultists. Once drunk on wine, they would work themselves into a degrading and orgiastic state to worship the false pagan god Dionysus. Paul is contrasting their trumped-up, wine-induced frenzies of religious exaltation with the sober, orderly, and controlled worship that being filled with the Spirit brings. The meaning of being filled with the Spirit, therefore, is not to get "drunk in the Spirit," but rather the very opposite. It is a call to discipline and self-control. These two ideas are mutually incompatible, not similar.[16]

The *Interpreter's Bible* states it this way: "The antithesis is not between wine and spirit but between the two states—intoxication with its degrading effects on the one hand; and a [sober] progressive fulfillment of the spiritual life on the other."[17]

Why Not "Drunk" in Acts 2:15 and Ephesians 5:18?

A highly speculative and faulty interpretation of being "drunk in the Spirit," based on taking Acts 2:15 and Ephesians 5:18 out of context, resulted in a blatant false teaching.

Consider Acts 2:15

Ten days after Christ's ascension, while the 120 were praying and worshipping the Lord in an upper room in Jerusalem, a mighty rushing wind came and tongues of fire rested on the heads of the 120. They were all filled with the Holy Spirit and began to speak with other tongues as the Spirit gave them utterance. So why did some in the crowd think the 120 were drunk?

Notice, it was not because they were staggering, falling down, or laughing uncontrollably in an inebriated state. The answer given in Acts 2:5–13 is this:

And there were dwelling at Jerusalem Jews, devout men, out of every nation under heaven. Now when this was noised abroad, the multitude came together, and were confounded, because that every man heard them speak in his own language. And they were all amazed and marvelled, saying one to another, Behold, are not all these which speak Galilaeans? And how hear we every man in our own tongue, wherein we were born? Parthians, and Medes, and Elamites, and the dwellers in Mesopotamia, and in Judaea, and Cappadocia, in Pontus, and Asia, Phrygia, and Pamphylia, in Egypt, and in the parts of Libya about Cyrene, and strangers of Rome, Jews and proselytes, Cretes and Arabians, we do hear them speak in our tongues the wonderful works of God. And they were all amazed, and were in doubt, saying one to another, What meaneth this? Others mocking said, These men are full of new wine.

Why was most of the multitude of devout men from every nation bewildered and amazed? Because they heard foreigners declaring the wonders of God, in their own tongues (Acts 2:5–12).

Notice, it was the mockers who said they had too much wine (Acts 2:13). The mockers, not the multitude, falsely accused the others of being drunk because, while some heard their own language, they also heard other languages. To the mockers this sounded like babbling, but the others were amazed and marveled (Acts 2:7, 12).

Also notice that Peter was able to preach a very accurate and powerful message (Acts 2:14–40)—something he could not have done if he had been inebriated.

Remember that those who were gathered were devout and God-fearing Jews who would not have listened to Peter if they thought he was drunk. But not only did they listen, many believed what he said and repented. In fact, following Peter's powerful message (which incidentally was filled with meaningful Scriptural content that appealed to reason) three thousand repented and were baptized (Acts 2:41).

Contrast this event with people who are "drunk in the Spirit"—who have difficulty testifying about what God has done for them and who often cannot speak, walk, or stand. Is this the fruit of the same Spirit who visited these men at Pentecost? Certainly not!

Furthermore, the testimonies given by proponents of "holy laughter" revolve around their experiences rather than around Jesus Christ and Scripture as Peter's sermon did.

Peter answered the mockers, "For these [men] are not drunken, as ye suppose" (Acts 2:15). He added, "But this is that which was spoken by the prophet Joel" (Acts 2:16).

Joel 2:28–32 (which Peter quoted from) states: "And it shall come to pass afterward, that I will pour out my spirit upon all flesh; and your sons and your daughters shall prophesy, your old men shall dream dreams, your young men shall see visions: And also upon the servants and upon the handmaids in those days will I pour out my spirit. And I will shew wonders in the heavens and in the earth, blood, and fire, and pillars of smoke. The sun shall be turned into darkness, and the moon into blood, before the great and terrible day of the LORD come. And it shall come to pass, that whosoever shall call on the name of the LORD shall be delivered..."

While many foolishly said, "Have a drink at Joel's place," Joel does not mention or suggest that drunken behavior is a sign of the outpouring of God's Spirit. Furthermore, there is no example anywhere in the New Testament of believers being "drunk in the Spirit." In fact, a fruit of the Spirit is self-control (Galatians 5:23) while one of the deeds of the flesh is drunkenness (Galatians 5:21).

Consider Ephesians

Ephesians 5:18 says, "And be not drunk with wine, wherein is excess; but be filled with the Spirit."

Being filled with the Spirit in this passage does not imply that one will experience some euphoric state of mind resulting in drunken behavior; quite the contrary, it is the antithesis of it. In the context of Ephesians 5, being filled with the Spirit means you are to let the Spirit so totally control you that you will live a life of obedience and discipline. This text in no way gives sanction to drunken-like behavior, of the so-called "drunk in the Spirit" enthusiasts.

The Wine of God's Wrath

"Intoxicating wine" and drunken behavior are often used in Scripture to signify God's wrath and judgment on a rebellious people:

Jeremiah 25:15, 16: "For thus saith the LORD God of Israel unto me; Take the wine cup of this fury at my hand, and cause all the nations, to whom I send thee, to drink it. And they shall drink, and be moved, and be mad, because of the sword that I will send among them."

Jeremiah 25:27–29: "Therefore thou shalt say unto them, Thus saith the LORD of hosts, the God of Israel; Drink ye, and be drunken, and spue, and fall, and rise no more, because of the sword which I will send among you. And it shall be, if they refuse to take the cup at thine hand to drink, then shalt thou say unto them, Thus saith the LORD of hosts; Ye shall certainly drink. For, lo, I begin to bring evil on the city which is called by my name, and should ye be utterly unpunished? Ye shall not be unpunished: for I will call for a sword upon all the inhabitants of the earth, saith the LORD of hosts."

Jeremiah 51:7: "Babylon hath been a golden cup in the LORD's hand, that made all the earth drunken: the nations have drunken of her wine; therefore the nations are mad."

Isaiah 51:17 : "Awake, awake, stand up, O Jerusalem, which hast drunk at the hand of the LORD the cup of his fury; thou hast drunken the dregs of the cup of trembling, and wrung them out."

Ezekiel 23:32, 33: "Thus saith the Lord GOD; Thou shalt drink of thy sister's cup deep and large: thou shalt be laughed to scorn and had in derision; it containeth much. Thou shalt be filled with drunkenness and sorrow, with the cup of astonishment and desolation, with the cup of thy sister Samaria."

Revelation 14:8: "And there followed another angel, saying, Babylon is fallen, is fallen, that great city, because she made all nations drink of the wine of the wrath of her fornication."

Revelation 17:1, 2, 6: "And there came one of the seven angels which had the seven vials, and talked with me, saying unto me, Come hither; I will shew unto thee the judgment of the great whore that sitteth upon many waters: With whom the kings of the earth have committed fornication, and the inhabitants of the earth have been made drunk with the wine of her fornication. And I saw the woman drunken with the blood of the saints, and with the blood of the martyrs of Jesus: and when I saw her, I wondered with great admiration."

Be Sober and on Guard

Anyone tempted to leave his mind at the door and "belly-on-up to the bar," needs to remember that the Spirit of God is the Spirit of truth. In order to receive truth the mind cannot be by-passed. When you release yourself to a mindless, intoxicated state, you are setting yourself up for vain imaginations or demonic delusions. You compromise your God-given responsibility to live soberly under the control of His Spirit. You surrender your biblical mandate to walk in discernment, wisdom, and understanding.

God is a God of order, not chaos. Just look around at His incredible creation. There is design, order, harmony, and restrained power. Compare this to the chaotic mess of the "drunken and disorderly conduct" of the "drunk-in-the-Spirit" crowd. You be the judge of who is the author of this confusion.

But consider this: Proponents of "holy laughter" and "being drunk in the Spirit" may be right when they say God is the one causing these phenomena to happen. We are told in 2 Thessalonians 2:10, 11 that God will send a strong delusion upon those who do not love the truth. It is becoming increasingly evident based on the recent phenomena crazes, "new revelations," and current trends that are so quickly being embraced by and welcomed into the church, that many do not have a love for the truth of God's Word!

Being "drunk in the Spirit" is definitely not a sign of the outpouring of God's Spirit, but is a fleshly, sometimes demonic behavior—often God's judgment on apostates.

Whatever Happened to the Word of God?

Returning to my observations regarding the "holy laughter" phenomenon that swept the church and the resulting bizarre behavior, let me add that it was not uncommon to see people lying flat on the floor as though they were stuck there with glue. In fact, proponents claimed that being unable to move or rise from the floor was caused by "Holy Ghost glue." Yet nowhere can we find the basis for this in the New Testament church, but being demonically controlled or frozen with fear is commonly manifested in the occult.

Although proponents of "holy laughter" admitted that these phenomena were very distracting and made what is being said from the pulpit irrelevant, they believed it was God who was doing the distracting so it was okay. But 1 Corinthians 14:33 plainly states, "For God is not the author of confusion, but of peace..." "Confusion" (*akatastasia*), according to *Vine's Expository Dictionary of New Testament Words,* "denotes a state of disorder, disturbance, tumult." 1 Corinthians 14:40 states, "Let all things be done decently and in order."

Proponents of "holy laughter" claimed to be receiving a new anointing accompanied by joy and a fresh outpouring of the Holy Spirit. They testified of having some of the most powerful services they ever experienced—changed lives and transformed congregations. Many claimed renewed faith, marriages, and ministries.

But the sad reality is that the fruit of all this unbiblical nonsense led to many church and ministry scandals, confused and split congregations, ruined lives and marriages, and a watching world once again repulsed by phenomena and behavior in Christ's name.

Those who endorsed "holy laughter" and related phenomena seldom gave Scripture to support their beliefs. If any Scripture references were given, they were taken out of context and given a twisted meaning. They gave a subjective reason—I experienced it, therefore it must be of God. Resorting to "human wisdom," they set aside the Word of God. Having no Scriptural basis, proponents of "holy laughter" claimed that God was doing a new work in His Church that goes beyond the Word of God.

Those drawn to these types of emotionally-driven services and ecstatic experiences were very often discouraged and depressed pastors or Christians who were burnt-out and felt powerless in their fruitless ministries. They turned to "holy laughter" and other strange, non-scriptural phenomena and teachings to revitalize their lives and ministries.

I wonder where their relationship was with the Christ of the Scriptures and their spiritual discernment, since many previously claimed to be Spirit-filled. How could such an inferior experience so powerfully affect and then shipwreck so many leaders in the church? But pastors and believers, hungry for the outpouring of God's Spirit, are becoming impatient and inadvertently accepting emotional and counterfeit experiences.

Many extreme groups started with people who got into false teaching by basing their beliefs on subjective experience rather than the Word of God. For example, a deeply religious man who taught Sunday school and read the Bible through once a year was unsure whether his psychic abilities came from God or the devil. But as a result of a personal experience, and with the urging of his family and friends, he began doing psychic healings. The result was a lifelong commitment to occult beliefs and phenomena which ended in physical, emotional, and spiritual devastation.

Also consider, much of the phenomena in Scripture that is often attributed to the demonic (struck dumb and unable to speak, uncontrollable shaking and convulsions, thrown around like a rag doll) was occurring to Christians and pastors.

Instead of reaching the world as the Lord's return draws closer, the "Church" was laughing uncontrollably, rolling around on the floor in convulsions, and struck dumb, unable to speak.

But the church is not laughing so much now as hard times have affected almost every believer and persecution on a world-wide scale is accelerating.

The Glory Fades

While ministering in Southern California several years after the "holy laughter" craze was fading, I wanted to know what the movement and leader were doing. During a break in my schedule I attended a five-hour service by the leader of the "holy laughter" movement.

There were many unbiblical manifestations and phenomena, as well as completely twisted words of Scripture. For example, when someone was laid out flat on the floor, supposedly struck by the Holy Spirit, the person rolled over. The leader quipped, "You may wonder what's happening, but God does not want us to be 'rare' or 'medium.' God wants us to be 'well done' on both sides, so we can be 'well done, good and faithful servant.'"

Other attendees at the meeting were literally struck dumb when they came forward to give testimony or to be prayed for. Many fell and were stuck like glue to the floor, much to the amusement of the audience and the leader. The leader said this is the prophesied revival sweeping the world. However, this hyper-emotional meeting was unimpressive and pathetic. It only reinforced how far some elements under the cloak of Christianity have gone in perverting the truth of the Bible.

What a far cry from New Testament Christianity and the power of God's Spirit manifested in the book of Acts.

A husband and wife told me about an evangelist who spoke at their church and advertised that there would be signs, wonders, and miracles. I asked this couple to give me examples of signs, wonders, and miracles in the Bible. They gave me an impressive listing. But then I asked, "And what signs, wonders, and miracles actually occurred through this evangelist?" They quickly acknowledged that his in no way even remotely compared to or resembled the biblical accounts.

"Peace" is Blissed-Out Meditative Trance

Proponents of "holy laughter" and related phenomena misused Scripture. Their method of biblical interpretation was faulty because they took verses out of context. Using their method I could easily take every text dealing with the word "peace" and, by their reasoning, justify the Eastern phenomenon of the "blissed-out meditative trance" and claim it is the work of the Holy Spirit. I could then go around the world conducting "holy peace" crusades and by my "holy touch" zap people into a nirvana-like state.

But why stop there? I could take the Scriptural references regarding bodily translation, like Enoch when he was translated into heaven, and Philip when he was translated out of the presence of the Ethiopian eunuch, and have people line up to have hands laid on them to be translated into heaven, another room, or another country.

Read All the Scriptures

The Scriptures given by "holy laughter" proponents (Job 5:22; 8:21; Psalm 16:11; 37:12, 13; 126:1, 2; Proverbs 15:13; Nehemiah 8:10; Acts 2:28; 3:19; etc) appeared on the surface to be biblical. But when each passage was checked in context, it was obvious they had been twisted and misapplied.

In these last days it is crucial that those who still endorse "holy laughter" and being "drunk in the Spirit" should also read a few more Scriptures.

Luke 21:34–36: "And take heed to yourselves, lest at any time your hearts be overcharged with surfeiting, and drunkenness, and cares of this life, and so that day come upon you unawares. For as a snare shall it come on all them that dwell on the face of the whole earth. Watch ye therefore, and pray always, that ye may be accounted worthy to escape all these things that shall come to pass, and to stand before the Son of man."

Romans 13:12–14: "The night is far spent, the day is at hand: let us therefore cast off the works of darkness, and let us put on the armour of light. Let us walk honestly, as in the day; not in rioting and drunkenness, not in chambering and wantonness, not in strife and envying. But put ye on the Lord Jesus Christ, and make not provision for the flesh, to fulfil the lusts thereof.

1 Peter 4:7: "But the end of all things is at hand: be ye therefore sober, and watch unto prayer."

1 Peter 5:8: "Be sober, be vigilant; because your adversary

the devil, as a roaring lion, walketh about, seeking whom he may devour."

Jeremiah 51:37–39: "And Babylon shall become heaps, a dwellingplace for dragons, an astonishment, and an hissing, without an inhabitant. They shall roar together like lions: they shall yell as lions' whelps. In their heat I will make their feasts, and I will make them drunken, that they may rejoice, and sleep a perpetual sleep, and not wake, saith the LORD."

Lay Hands on No Man Suddenly

1 Timothy 5:22 states, "Lay hands suddenly on no man, neither be partaker of other men's sins: keep thyself pure." So too, we must be cautious whom we permit to lay hands on us. Once you go up front for an evangelist, prophet, or apostle to pray for you, you have submitted to them. You are now vulnerable to be influenced by what, or who they represent. If they are propagating non-biblical beliefs or techniques, or demonic powers, that could be as potentially dangerous as submitting to someone in an occult meeting.

I believe that Christians who submit to being "slain in the Spirit," "holy laughter," and other unbiblical, oftentimes occult phenomena are in the same spiritual danger as those who attend séances or play with Ouija boards. Many have experienced the same physical, mental, emotional, and spiritual oppression that those who dabble in the occult eventually do.

It is also interesting that the same spirit I encountered through spiritual warfare and confronting witches, spiritualists, mediums, Satanists, and New Agers for twenty years is now manifest in the Church.

Resembles Hindu Occultism

The phenomena of being "slain in the Spirit" and "holy laughter" are about as impressive and Scriptural as Guru Maharaj Ji's techniques, which supposedly enabled his adherents to see the "Divine light of God," hear the "Divine music of God," feel the "Word of God in their flesh," and taste the "Divine nectar of God."

According to researcher Ellis Stewart's article on *Hindu Occultism:*

> The most feared and revered deity in Hinduism is the goddess Kali (Durga), the wife of Shiva the destroyer. She is also known as Shakti, which means "force," and represents the impersonal force that occultism teaches runs the universe. The divine power-touch of the guru is called shaktipat. This is a term used for the touch (or near touch) of a guru's hand to the worshipper's forehead that produces supernatural effects. Shakti literally means power; and in administering the shaktipat the guru becomes a channel of primal power, the cosmic power (so they believe) underlying the universe. The supernatural effect of shakti through the guru's touch may knock the worshiper to the floor or he may see a bright light and receive an experience of enlightenment or inner illumination, or have some other mystical or psychic experience.[18]

Pastor Catapulted From Chair

A magazine article by proponents of "holy laughter" boasted of a pastor, who while quietly weeping and worshiping, was suddenly catapulted from his chair. He flew through the air nearly ten feet down the aisle, landing on his face. If this were really so, does it even remotely resemble the Holy Spirit in the Bible? But it does resemble demonic manifestations in the occult.

While talking to some leaders at the church in Toronto promoting the "Toronto blessing," I asked, "How far can this phenomena go before you say 'enough is enough'?" One of them immediately responded, "You are being judgmental. This conversation is terminated." I replied, "I am not being judgmental. I am just trying to find a biblical basis for your endorsement of this supposed outpouring of God's Spirit." But they refused to even discuss it.

On another occasion a man I know who was at one time in leadership at his church, was physically escorted out of the church because he questioned the pastor concerning the Scriptural basis of his teaching. There also have been many prophecies and pronouncements of destruction on those who oppose—and sometimes on those who merely don't go along with—their aberrant teachings and practices.

The Israelites of Gideon's day had become so corrupt they were going to kill Gideon because he had broken down Baal's altar and had cut down the Asherah pole beside it (Judges 6:30). Are "Christian" leaders today becoming so corrupt that not only do they tolerate energy forces and familiar spirits masquerading as the Holy Spirit, but they seek to destroy, through prophetic utterance or other means, those who biblically expose ("cut down") the unbiblical phenomena in the church?

In the occult, the main focus is subjective experience and phenomena, with little regard for doctrine and truth. Ironically, the church today focuses on feelings and experiences that make you feel good, with little concern for Scriptural truth.

It Is a Sad Day

It is sad indeed that those for whom Christ died and whom He has called to be His Bride are so far removed from biblical Christianity. Many have become spiritual prostitutes. Once I dreamed the Lord was speaking through me to a group of people who were embracing false teaching and phenomena. I said to them: "How diabolical that something which is not even in Scripture is causing so many church splits, divisions, and turmoil in the body of Christ." Historically, most heresies and divisions in the church have started with at least some aspect of Scripture. But much error today has absolutely no basis in God's Word, yet it divides many churches.

Christians who embrace subjective experiences rather than the objective, inspired Word of God, will consequently involve themselves in even more bizarre manifestations they attribute to the Holy Spirit. Some of this behavior in these last days, I am convinced, will involve outright sexual immorality and blatant demonic activity around the very altar. Unless they repent they will suffer dire consequences as they find the Lord "fighting against them" (Revelation 2:16).

God sent Judah into Babylonian captivity because the people and leaders would not respond to His discipline and instruction but turned their backs to Him and set up their abominations in the house that bears His name and defiled it (Jeremiah 32:32–34). Far worse today are pastors and leaders who defile the Church which He redeemed with His blood, by allowing New Age, occult practices and techniques—and believers' bodies, temples of the Holy Spirit, participating in detestable phenomena and practices.

Reflects the Occult More than the Scriptural Norm

Many claim that various phenomena such as falling down, laughing, shaking, jerking, and jumping up and down uncontrollably, convulsions, feelings of warmth and electricity, and other such experiences occur when the Holy Spirit comes on a person. However, these behavior and sensations far more resemble self-induced experiences or the occult than they represent the norm in Scripture of God's Spirit moving in a person's life.

The Holy Spirit "is not energy or electricity or anything that any human being can pump, scoop, blow, charge with, or press into another person. The Holy Spirit is God. Even when we speak of the 'power' of the Holy Spirit, this is not some energy... [Energy] is a New Age concept, not a biblical one."[19]

The desire to turn off the mind, lose control of oneself, and have euphoric experiences, are primary characteristics of occultism and Eastern mysticism—not biblical Christianity. For example, in an issue of SCP Newsletter, a quote was included from the book, *The Stormy Search for the Self,* in which the New Age authors state: "During powerful rushes of Kundalini energy, [individuals] often emit various involuntary sounds, and their bodies move in strange and unexpected patterns. Among the most common manifestations...are unmotivated and unnatural laughter or crying...and imitating a variety of animal sounds and movements."[20]

You might say, "The atmosphere was positive and very exciting, and everyone seemed warm and friendly. I felt great and so close to the Lord that it had to be the Holy Spirit." Well, I have been in many occult and New Age meetings and believe me, they are very positive. There is electricity in the air and there is a great excitement and expectancy of what "God" is going to do.

The former Oregon guru, Bhagwhan Shree Rajneesh, was often referred to as being "drunk on the divine." He would draw his followers to himself and ask them to "drink" from him. His spiritual "wine" could be obtained by merely a touch of his hand to the head. After his touch many would fall to the floor in ecstasy.[21]

Ramakrishna, an Indian saint, daily went into "samadhi," a trance-like stupor, "in which one involuntarily falls down unconscious and enters a rapturous state of super-conscious bliss (ananda)... These states could last anywhere from a few minutes to several days and were often accompanied by uncontrollable laughter or weeping. He could send others into this state with a single touch to the head or chest."[22]

Swami Baba Muktananda "would transfer what was called 'guru's grace' to his followers through Shaktipat (physical touch). This 'grace' triggered the gradual awakening of the Kundalini, which in turn produced various physical and emotional manifestations. Manifestations included uncontrollable laughing, roaring, barking, hissing, crying, shaking, etc. Some devotees became mute or unconscious. Many felt themselves being infused with feelings of great joy and peace and love. At other times the 'fire' of Kundalini was so overpowering they would find themselves involuntarily hyperventilating to cool themselves down."[23]

During the 1960s and 1970s, the massive influence of Eastern mysticism and occult practices drew the Western world into a feelings-oriented frenzy. Devotees rejected the cold orthodoxy of the established church for the more subjective emotional experience of gurus and shamans. No longer was validation based on the external, objective Word of God, but rather on internal, subjective impulses. Reason was cast aside like some old tattered garment. The cultural cry of that age, "If it feels good—do it," penetrated the Church.

But how you *feel* can never be the ultimate criterion for evaluating phenomena and experiences. Proper interpretation of Scripture, or in other words, rightly dividing the Word of Truth, is where we must always begin and end in determining how we walk in this world, which will offer an increasing plethora of mystical experiences until Christ returns.

Do Not Be Impressed by Phenomena...

So-called miracles, healings, prophecies, revelations, and other such phenomena by themselves should not impress us. My staff and I witnessed them occur in various cult, occult, Eastern mystical, and New Age groups we researched.

Many Christians go to a meeting, and because the Bible is used or the name of Jesus is mentioned, they accept everything that happens as being from God. Yet, I have researched séances and spiritualist meetings and attended many occult and New Age gatherings where they quoted the Bible, talked about Jesus and even raised their hands to supposedly praise Him. Some actually professed to be Spirit-filled Christians living under His Lordship. Many Hindu gurus and practitioners of black magic and occultism use Scripture and invoke the name of Jesus in an attempt to validate their beliefs and practices.

Bring in the Fortune-Tellers and Mediums

I am convinced that in many Christian circles, mediums, channelers, and fortune-tellers could come in, and if they prayed in

Jesus' name, or raised their hands to praise Jesus or quoted a few Scriptures and then operated their "gifts," most in attendance would not even know the difference and would believe it was the Holy Spirit.

Johanna Michaelsen believes in the gifts of the Holy Spirit. In her book, *The Beautiful Side of Evil,* she warns believers to discern the gifts because, as she says, "We shouldn't be too surprised to find practicing occultists within most of our denominations…"

She goes on to say:

For example, believers with occultic backgrounds which have never been renounced are manifesting mediumistic gifts and techniques which go undiscerned in the atmosphere of ecstatic hoopla which frequently characterizes so many meetings…

Mediumistic gifts can, but do not always, automatically disappear when one becomes a believer. Mine didn't. I was more psychic than ever…and from what I've seen in many of our meetings, my abilities would have been acclaimed as the gift of "words of knowledge" and "prophecy." It was actually clairvoyance.

It was not until I took the *offensive* in my ongoing battle against Satan, making a *full* list of *all* my sins… renouncing them and all the works and gifts of Satan, and then *totally* refraining from practicing these things, that these psychic powers faded over a period of months. It has been so with many others whom I've counseled. I truly believe that those with occultic backgrounds should wait a season before seeking and exercising any of the more spectacular gifts of the Spirit until they have matured in the grace and knowledge of the Lord.[24]

The Occult Connection

I went to a meeting to hear a female evangelist who supposedly operated all the gifts of the Holy Spirit. But after hearing her, I was convinced she was either operating in the flesh or by a demonic spirit—definitely not by the Spirit of God.

It was unbelievable how all these alleged born-again, Spirit-filled Christians ran up front to be "slain in the Spirit," have hands laid on them for healing, and to be prophesied over. They played her tapes over and over before going to bed, so they could listen to every word she had from the Lord for them. But as I talked to these Christians, I was appalled at their immaturity, their ignorance of God's Word, and their lack of discernment.

The female evangelist, whom they practically worshiped, gave several false prophecies and many unimpressive "miracles." She called forward an older lady and told her that the reason she always had a sad face was because she had a glandular problem. Before praying for her, she assured her that she would go back to her seat healed and with a smile. Again she was wrong, as the sad-faced lady went back to her seat unchanged. Later, I learned that her saddened condition was due to the recent deaths of her husband and son and was not caused by a glandular problem.

It seemed that no matter what problem anyone had, her solution was for them to go forward, receive a few words of prophecy and a prayer for healing, be "slain in the Spirit," and everything would be okay—but it wasn't. I knew in my spirit that this evangelist had been involved in the occult before supposedly becoming a Christian. The same false prophecies, the same Scripture-twisting, and the same spiritual warfare I had encountered while interviewing, researching, and witnessing to fortune-tellers and mediums, I experienced in dealing with this evangelist.

I told my research director that if I could get a taped interview with her (something she had refused to do), I could prove that somewhere in her past there was an occult connection. Even though several people had finally realized what I was saying was true and left her group, no one was able or willing to show me the "occult connection" in her background.

Finally, after several years of opposition from members of this group, a woman who heard me on the radio called and said, "I can confirm something for you. I know a former neighbor of this lady, and she was, in fact, a fortune-teller before." I said, "That is what the Holy Spirit impressed on my heart years before. That is what I knew from God's Word and Spirit, and my research, and now you are finally confirming it." She nevertheless continued to operate her fortune-telling gift under the guise of Christianity—duping her foolish followers, until the day she died.

Discerning Demonic Counterfeits

A woman from out of state called for help for a man she knew. During our conversation, she began to speak in tongues to impress me with the fact that she had been filled with the Spirit. But I discerned her tongues to be counterfeit. She told me she was baptized in the Spirit. I said, "You must really be hungry for God's Word and reading it every day." She said, "Oh, no! I don't have time or the need to read it anymore. Jesus often appears and speaks directly to me now."

There is an increasing "demonic connection" as more and more supposed Christians are either experiencing or manifesting demonic phenomena. Just as there are tragic consequences for those who become involved in the occult—physically, mentally, emotionally, and spiritually—so too, I am seeing a pattern of resulting tragedies manifest in the lives of many "Christians" who are ignorantly or purposely becoming involved in occult and New Age techniques, practices, and beliefs being taught in their churches.

In the day and age we live, even if what is said or written seems good on the surface, sounds Scriptural, and seems to exalt Jesus, we must remember, the following Scriptural accounts:

1) In Luke 4:34, a demon-possessed man cried out to Jesus, "I know who You are—the Holy One of God!"
2) During his temptation of Jesus, recorded in Matthew 4:1–11, Satan quoted Scripture, but subtly twisted its meaning.
3) In Acts 16:16–18, we read an account of a slave-girl who had a spirit of divination. She followed after Paul and kept crying out, "These men are the servants of the most high God, which shew unto us the way of salvation." Paul's response was to cast the spirit out.

2 Kings 17:33, 41 states: "They feared the LORD, and served their own gods, after the manner of the nations whom they carried away from thence. So these nations feared the LORD, and served their graven images, both their children, and their children's children: as did their fathers, so do they unto this day."

The Spirit of Simon the Sorcerer

Many today are seeking to use the Holy Spirit for spiritual power and personal advancement.

Acts 8:18–22 records: "And when Simon saw that through laying on of the apostles' hands the Holy Ghost was given, he offered them money, Saying, Give me also this power, that on whomsoever I lay hands, he may receive the Holy Ghost. But Peter said unto him, Thy money perish with thee, because thou hast thought that the gift of God may be purchased with money. Thou hast neither part nor lot in this matter: for thy heart is not right in the sight of God. Repent therefore of this thy wickedness, and pray God, if perhaps the thought of thine heart may be forgiven thee."

The same spirit of Simon is manifest in many believers and Christian leaders today as they are seeking power to perform signs and wonders, not just to advance the Gospel, but for their own ulterior motives.

While Peter would not offer the gift of the Holy Spirit for financial gain, many supposed Christian leaders are more than willing to "sell" Him to gullible followers.

The False Prophet Deceives the World With "Miracles"

How does the False Prophet deceive those who dwell on the earth? Revelation 13:14 answers: "And deceiveth them that dwell on the earth by the means of those miracles which he had power to do in the sight of the beast; saying to them that dwell on the earth, that they should make an image to the beast, which had the wound by a sword, and did live."

Revelation 13:13 says: "And he doeth great wonders, so that he maketh fire come down from heaven on the earth in the sight of men."

Paul tells us about this in 2 Thessalonians 2:8, 9: "And then shall that Wicked be revealed, whom the Lord shall consume with the spirit of his mouth, and shall destroy with the brightness

NOT OUR FATHER'S FAITH

of his coming: Even him, whose coming is after the working of Satan with all power and signs and lying wonders."

Revelation 16:13, 14 states: "And I saw three unclean spirits like frogs come out of the mouth of the dragon, and out of the mouth of the beast, and out of the mouth of the false prophet. For they are the spirits of devils, working miracles, which go forth unto the kings of the earth and of the whole world, to gather them to the battle of that great day of God Almighty."

Revelations 19:20 says: "And the beast was taken, and with him the false prophet that wrought miracles before him, with which he deceived them that had received the mark of the beast, and them that worshipped his image. These both were cast alive into a lake of fire burning with brimstone."

We are living at a time of great deception, and Scripture strongly indicates it is going to accelerate. I am convinced that many Christians who live by the experiential, who follow signs and wonders, who lack discernment, and who do not rightly divide the Word of Truth are being deceived by a great delusion Paul prophesied would overtake those who reject a love for the truth (2 Thessalonians 2:10). And if so many are being deceived now, how do they expect to stand when the deception gets even more difficult to discern as the very incarnation of Satan comes on the scene, and numerous amazing false miracles, signs, and wonders occur?

A Sobering Warning From Christ

Jesus says in Matthew 7:20, "Wherefore by their fruits ye shall know them"—not by their gifts or power or miracles. Satan can counterfeit the gifts of the Spirit, but he cannot duplicate the genuine fruit of the Spirit.

Jesus went on in Matthew 7:21–23 to give one of the most startling concepts in Scripture: "Not every one that saith unto me, Lord, Lord, shall enter into the kingdom of heaven; but he that doeth the will of my Father which is in heaven. Many will say to me in that day, Lord, Lord, have we not prophesied in thy name? and in thy name have cast out devils? and in thy name done many wonderful works? And then will I profess unto them, I never knew you: depart from me, ye that work iniquity."

These people used biblical terminology. They called Him Lord. They supposedly prophesied in His name, performed miracles in His name, and cast out demons in His name, but that is not the validation. As much as we need the gifts of the Spirit in our lives and ministries, that is not the criterion for receiving His approval.

Jesus will not say, "I knew you because you prophesied in My name, because you cast out demons in My name, or because you did miracles in My name." No! If that is the basis of why you think He should welcome you into His kingdom, then you may be surprised when he says to you, "Depart from Me, I never knew you."

The requirement is knowing Him personally and, "He who does the will of My Father who is in heaven." That is why I am not impressed by the phenomena that go on. What is really important is that you *know* the Jesus of the Bible in a real and intimate way, that He is *truly* Lord of your life, that you are walking in obedience to His Word and Spirit, that you are being conformed to His image, that your heart's desire is to exalt and glorify Him, that you are bearing fruit for His glory, and the fruit of the Spirit is being manifested in your life!

Former "Head-hunters" Seek the Real Thing

I ministered at a national convention in the Himalayas in India to people coming out of backgrounds of Hinduism, Buddhism, idolatry, spiritism, ancestor worship, demon worship, sorcery, witchcraft, and various other forms of mysticism and occultism. These people, some of whom were former witch-doctors and "head-hunters," did not want to be influenced by mere hype, emotionalism, and imitations of the Holy Spirit—or by any counterfeit techniques.

In some of the mountain villages, many of these people pay a great price to live for Christ. They are forsaken by families and friends and are spit on, stoned, and beaten with bamboo sticks for witnessing and speaking about Christ. Before I spoke the first time I was told that these people would evaluate everything I said by Scripture—and it had better be accurate. God greatly honored His Word and anointed each service. After every message, hundreds came to the altar where God moved on hearts in a powerful way.

It is ironic to me that so many Christians are settling for inferior and counterfeit experiences and are involving themselves in the beliefs, practices, and techniques that these people renounced when they came to Christ. Having come out of a background of mysticism and occultism, these people are seeking to live a New Testament Christianity, and are seeing God move in powerful ways.

Refuse to Settle for Less than the Genuine

There are three main problems with the current trends and phenomena in many Christian circles. First, they are unsupported by

God's Word. Second, they are found rooted in the occult, Eastern mysticism, and the New Age movement. And third, the phenomena and "miracles" are blatantly inferior to that which is recorded in Scripture.

I want everything God has, but I refuse to settle for an imitation or a counterfeit. Before I can receive the genuine, I have to be honest. The power does not come from me, nor do I control when or how it operates. Gimmickry must not be tolerated nor New Age techniques, mind control, or mass hypnosis used. I cannot camouflage the "power of ki/ch'i" (impersonal energy force) as the Holy Spirit. I cannot try to pass off a "spirit guide" as the Holy Spirit. I cannot resort to emotion and hype and say, "This is the Holy Spirit." I cannot push on your head and knock you down or work you into an emotional frenzy and exclaim, "See how God's Spirit is moving." I cannot use psychosomatic healing techniques and claim they are God's supernatural power.

We will not receive the genuine outpouring of His Spirit if we embrace gimmickry, manifestations of flesh, and counterfeits, or utilize any other technique in an attempt to deceive ourselves, or others into believing it is the Holy Spirit.

The Lord is calling the body of Christ to integrity! We cannot hide behind a smoke screen of superficial spirituality. We must not settle for anything less than the genuine moving of the Holy Spirit.

From my research into the last days, the New Age movement, the current trends infiltrating the Church, and from my study of God's Word and the witness of His Spirit through many hours of prayer and fasting, I am convinced that we are in the midst of the prophesied apostasy and deception. I also believe we are on the verge of a genuine outpouring of and empowering by God's Spirit before Christ's Second Coming. That is why Satan is raising up so much imitation and counterfeit. I believe those who stay faithful to the Jesus of the Bible and the Word of God will be supernaturally empowered by His Spirit. In the midst of persecution we will see the resurrection power of Christ as manifested in the book of Acts and in the prophesies of Joel chapter 2—as well as an increase of the imitation and counterfeit.

That is why I am saying, "Beware. Be alert." That is why I am challenging you to develop discernment by knowing the Word of God and knowing the God of the Word. That is why we must continually seek Him with all our heart, mind, soul, and strength.

When the Spirit of God comes upon you, He doesn't make you fall over, stagger, act like a drunk, be struck dumb, or manifest other bizarre and useless displays of "power." No. When the Spirit empowers you, He gives you faith, courage, boldness, strength, power, anointing, authority, peace, joy, love, self-control, perseverance, and wisdom, and all that is needed to share the Gospel, be a powerful witness, live a godly life, and accomplish all that He has called you to do.

Seek Him

Those who seek the Lord daily with their whole heart through His Word, prayer, and fasting will know Him. They will not settle for imitation, counterfeit, and inferior power, signs, and wonders, for they will walk in discernment, and the true power of the resurrected Christ will be manifested in their lives. Initially their power might not seem as impressive, but in the end it will prove far superior, for it is derived from the one true God, His Son, Jesus Christ, and the transforming work of His Holy Spirit.

True revival and the outpouring of God's Spirit is not the

result of man's manipulation or leaders showing off their supposed power and gifts. It is God's sovereign intervention in response to those who in humility and brokenness seek the Lord with all their hearts, pray, fast, and purify their lives.

True revival will come when believers hunger and thirst for the Jesus of the Bible, as a drowning man desires a breath of fresh air. When we desire Him more than anything else we will see Him move in powerful ways.

As committed Christians we need to always use discernment, stay true to God's Word, maintain a testimony for the Jesus of the Bible, and walk in the genuine power of His Spirit.

Chapter Eight

APOSTASY NOW!—COMING SOON TO A CHURCH NEAR YOU

A s I watched several "Christian" television programs, I witnessed both subtle and blatant Scripture-twisting as well as unbiblical phenomena. I was grieved in spirit and said to my wife, "It is as though we are seeing right before our eyes the apostate church and whore of Babylon who will help bring about the temporary reign of the Antichrist."

The deception, fakery, greed, and immorality surfacing in the body of Christ is just the tip of the iceberg. God is exposing many who are merchandising the Gospel and living in immorality. Only those walking before Him in truth and integrity will be standing when it is all over!

Judgment Begins with the House of God

The Lord is searching the heart and examining the lifestyle of each pastor, Christian leader, and believer. If you are tolerating anything contrary to His Word or Spirit, now is the time to repent and be faithful in all things. Let all who name His name strive in every way to live and proclaim biblical Christianity.

1 Peter 4: 17 states: "For the time is come that judgment must begin at the house of God: and if it first begin at us, what shall the end be of them that obey not the gospel of God?"

Impending judgment is facing the entire world but first the Lord is dealing with His Church.

As religious shysters are exposed, many Christians are having their eyes opened. Funds once given to fake ministries to build exorbitant kingdoms and personal estates will hopefully be directed to genuine ministries and churches to help get the true Gospel to all the world before our Lord's return.

Jude 3–7

In light of increasing deception in the Church and world, let's examine several timely verses in the book of Jude. Scripture is printed in bold with my comments in brackets.

Jude 3–7 states:

Beloved, when I gave all diligence to write unto you of the common salvation,

[I, too, would much rather only write about our salvation in Christ.]

it was needful for me to write unto you, and exhort you that ye should earnestly contend for the faith which was once delivered unto the saints.

[We are living in a day and age when we must boldly stand for the faith—not some "new revelation" or watered-down Gospel.]

For there are certain men crept in unawares, who were before of old ordained to this condemnation, ungodly men, turning the grace of our God into lasciviousness, and denying the only Lord God, and our Lord Jesus Christ.

[They appeared to be ministers and prophets of Christ, but they are ravenous wolves. They profess with their mouth Jesus is Lord and praise Him with their lips, but their pleasure-oriented lifestyles and exchanging the fruit of the Spirit for the lusts of the flesh, prove they deny Him as Lord in their hearts.]

I will therefore put you in remembrance, though ye once knew this, how that the Lord, having saved the people out of the land of Egypt, afterward destroyed them that believed not. And the angels which kept not their first estate, but left their own habitation, he hath reserved in everlasting chains under darkness unto the judgment of the great day. Even as Sodom and Gomorrha, and the cities about them in like manner, giving themselves over to fornication, and going after strange flesh, are set forth for an example, suffering the vengeance of eternal fire.

[God's judgment will eventually fall on those who refuse to believe, pervert His truth, and lead His people astray.]

Jude 8, 9

Jude 8 and 9 continues:

Likewise also these filthy dreamers defile the flesh, despise dominion, and speak evil of dignities.

[They are dreamers because all their unbiblical revelations keep them out of touch with the truth and reality of God's Word. They pollute their bodies with all their greed and immorality. They reject authority by refusing to let anyone correct the error of their ways. They arrogantly rant and rave against Satan and pretend to stomp him under their feet.]

Yet Michael the archangel, when contending with the devil he disputed about the body of Moses, durst not bring against him a railing accusation, but said, The Lord rebuke thee.

Jude 10–13

Jude 10–13 goes on to say concerning them:

But these speak evil of those things which they know not: but what they know naturally, as brute beasts, in those things they corrupt themselves.

Woe unto them! for they have gone in the way of Cain,

[Just as Cain killed his brother Abel, so these false teachers poison their followers by offering them a tainted Gospel.]

and ran greedily after the error of Balaam for reward,

[Just as Balaam was motivated by greed and personal gain to seduce the children of Israel from pure devotion to the Lord, so these false teachers seduce many from pure devotion to Christ.]

and perished in the gainsaying of Core.

[Their destruction is as sure as Korah's who was judged for his rebellion before the Lord. The days of these false teachers and false prophets are numbered. They will ultimately be exposed and destroyed.]

These are spots in your feasts of charity, when they feast with you,

[They are controlled by the cravings of their sensual appetites rather than hungering and thirsting for the Lord.]

feeding themselves without fear:

[Instead of feeding their flock the Word of Truth, they merchandise the Gospel for personal gain and to feed their own fleshly desires.]

clouds they are without water, carried about of winds;

[Just as clouds without rain deceive a parched land into thinking it will get life-giving moisture, so too, these false teachers deceive their followers into thinking they are giving them the genuine Bread from Heaven. They are blown from one new trend or teaching to the next.]

trees whose fruit withereth, without fruit, twice dead, plucked up by the roots; Raging waves of the sea, foaming out their own shame;

[They are spiritually dead now and will soon face the second death in the lake of fire. God exposes the true motives of these false teachers just as the waves turn up debris from the ocean floor and leave it lying on the beach for all to see. Their motivation is not ministry, but pleasure, power, and prosperity.]

wandering stars, to whom is reserved the blackness of darkness for ever.

[Shooting like meteorites across the sky, they come on the scene and rapidly rise to prominence with their "new revelations" and phenomena, but their glory is usually short-lived. Their eternal destiny is terrifying because they did not heed the Scriptural warning that teachers will be judged more strictly—James 3:1.]

Jude 17-20

Jude 17–20 concludes:

But, beloved, remember ye the words which were spoken before of the apostles of our Lord Jesus Christ; How that they told you there should be mockers in the last time, who should walk after their own ungodly lusts.

[False teachers scoff at the truth and fulfill their sensual desires as they tickle the ears of their listeners. False doctrine, not sound teaching, is what causes division in the church.]

These be they who separate themselves, sensual, having not the Spirit.

[They claim to be the spiritual elite, but they lack spiritual discernment. They speak from their own inspiration because they do not have the Holy Spirit.]

But ye, beloved, building up yourselves on your most holy faith, praying in the Holy Ghost.

[The truth as revealed in God's Word, is our source of strength and what builds our faith. Pray that you may be able to walk in discernment in these last days and in the genuine power of God's Spirit.]

Too Many Fakes—So What Do We Do?

Most people are impressed by external appearance. They hear a dynamic speaker, view a touching media presentation, see masses of enthralled and cheering people, and blindly get caught up in the emotion and excitement of the moment or the movement.

The pages of history are laced with accounts of multitudes being led astray by charismatic personalities, supposedly new trends, seemingly noble causes, but deceptive motives. The Hitler youth movement influenced a generation, changed a nation, and impacted the world. One day a dynamic political leader and an influential religious leader will arise. They will have great charisma, persuasive speech, hypnotizing words, miraculous powers, and incredible influence; but their true intents will be concealed with intrigue and deception. They will lead a world of undiscerning people down a path of global and eternal destruction. Our world is ripe for such political and religious world leaders.

It is imperative we look beyond the surface. Many times when the layers of glitz and glamour are peeled away, what remains is shockingly different from what was professed and presented. Whether it is a politician or a preacher, we need discernment.

Let me give you an example of how easy it is to get caught up in the hype and excitement of a cause or movement.

- As a teen in the late 1960's I saw many get caught up in the race riots and rebellion against authority and the establishment, without ever even considering why or where this movement was headed. Very few of my peers really thought about the reason why we were involved or where it would lead. We just went with the flow and growing enthusiasm and joined the crowd for a dead-end ride.

  Then as a new Christian I had to learn the lesson of discernment and integrity. The following are just a few examples how I learned early on about the fakery and hypocrisy that sometimes goes on in the name of Christ.

- A popular evangelist who amazed young and old alike with Bible prophecy had a part in my coming to faith in Christ. A short time later he left his wife and ran off with his secretary, became an alcoholic, embezzled ministry funds, and eventually spent time in prison. As a new Christian I had to make a crucial choice: Do I build my life on men or on God? I chose to build my life and ministry on Christ and His Word and that has made all the difference.

- A popular Christian group performed at a large camp meeting I attended as a new Christian. They sang and testified and shared stories with tears that moved the audience into emotional euphoria. I am not sure why I was never that impressed but I am glad I was not. A few years later they went secular and began singing some raunchy songs. It was hard for me to understand then how they could sing about Jesus with such passion, and then so quickly turn and for money deny the Lord and sing about things that led young people and adults down a path away from Him. It was not surprising to learn shortly thereafter that when they had been doing the Christian circuit, following many of their concerts, they were having sex with girls and women who attended their concerts.

- As a young Christian I attended a large service by a famous female evangelist. There was an atmosphere of expectancy, but I felt it was more hype than Holy Spirit. I got dragged up to the stage by several people I was with. They and hundreds of others fell down as she breezed past or touched them on the forehead. After several touches on my head, I was the only one on stage, except her, left standing. I was open and hungry for everything of God, just not willing to follow the crowd blindly and succumb to peer pressure, wanting rather to keep my eyes and allegiance on Him.

I could share countless illustrations of faked healings, false words from the Lord, financial misappropriation, sexual immorality, drug and alcohol usage, and much more. Some could be understood as the weakness of vessels of flesh. However, much was defiantly flaunted in God's face and willfully mocked the Lord and His people who enabled them to live such a lifestyle because of their lack of discernment and knowledge of God's Word.

So What Do We Do?

Does all the fakery and hypocrisy mean we should reject Christ and Christianity? To the contrary, we should embrace Him all the more because His Word warns about such people and practices. I have spent more than half a lifetime getting to know the Lord and discovering His reality and faithfulness. Besides, where is there to go if I reject the God who created me? He alone has the answers to eternal life.

And why deceive His people when it is a certain fact that I will give an account to Him for every word I speak, every thought and action, and the motives of my heart?

Without a doubt there are many cons that come in the name of Christ, as well as many supposed leaders who are as deceived as the people who follow them. Nevertheless, I have met countless pastors, missionaries, chaplains, and believers who are genuine. They love the Lord with all their hearts and the fruit of their ministries and personal sacrifices—both in front of people and behind the scenes—validates their testimonies of commitment and faithfulness to Him. They are mere mortals, but their beliefs and lifestyles prove they serve an immortal God.

I am also meeting a growing number of believers who, in spite of the world becoming more and more vile and corrupt, are desiring with all their hearts to walk in faithfulness and holiness before the Lord. They know His coming is at hand and judgment is about to fall on this world and they want to be faithful servants when He comes or they go to be with Him.

It will not be fun to meet the Lord as a false or unfaithful servant. "It is a fearful thing to fall into the hands of the living God" (Hebrews 10:31).

What we need in this day and age—whether it is in religious circles or the political arena—is discernment. We must not be impressed, influenced, or seduced by mere words or surface appearance of those who have ulterior motives and agendas.

We live at a time when we must have a personal and intimate relationship with the Lord, know the voice of His Spirit, obey the truth and principles of His Word, and walk in love, integrity, and self-control. Although the days are becoming increasingly confusing and corrupt, those who truly know the Lord will have wisdom and insight and will do exploits in His name.

Today We Need

There is so much in God's Word that we barely scratch its surface. We need leaders who will delve into the Scriptures and allow God's Spirit to give them insight so they can make known the deep riches of His Word. We need leaders who will sacrifice for the sake of the Gospel the way our Lord and His disciples did. We need those who will walk in integrity and the genuine power of the Holy Spirit. We need those who will proclaim the pure Word of God under the anointing of His Spirit.

Chapter Nine

A SPECIAL CHALLENGE TO THE BODY OF CHRIST!

Through this book and in many other ways, I have warned about deception and apostasy in the body of Christ and issued a call to return to biblical Christianity.

Junk Food Diet Spiritually

We are seeing a famine for the Word of God in our generation. A prophet of old had words to say about this very thing. Amos 8:11, 12 warns: "Behold, the days come, saith the Lord GOD, that I will send a famine in the land, not a famine of bread, nor a thirst for water, but of hearing the words of the LORD: And they shall wander from sea to sea, and from the north even to the east, they shall run to and fro to seek the word of the LORD, and shall not find it."

Children eat all the junk food they can get, because it tastes so good. They live in the "now," so they are not concerned about the resulting consequences of malnutrition and susceptibility to other adverse consequences such as stomachaches, rotten teeth, and obesity.

Many Christians are doing the same by living on a junk food diet spiritually. All they want is the excitement and blessing without the responsibility, commitment, and discipline. As a result, they are spiritually malnourished and susceptible to false doctrine.

The lack of knowledge of the Word and the lack of discernment manifested by many "Christian" leaders and their followers is appalling.

I heard someone say the following about one of these teachers who, I think, is very extreme and unbiblical. They said, "I listened hour after hour for over fifty hours to this person's tapes and I was so full of God's Word that I was just exploding." I thought to myself, *All you got filled with was that person's "interpretation" of God's Word.*

If this person had spent those fifty hours in God's Word, he would have been much better off. Many hold these teachers and prophets in higher esteem than they hold Jesus Christ, and listen to their tapes and read their books more than they study the Bible—and this should not be so.

As much as I hope you will read my books and listen to my CDs, do so with an open Bible. Do not let my words be the foundation of your spiritual diet. Spend more time in God's Word. Far more important than anything I say or anyone else says is a commitment from you to get into Scripture and seeking the Lord with all your heart.

Zen Koan

There is a thing in Zen Buddhism called a *koan*. A koan is a para-dox or insoluble problem that you meditate on with the intent to derail your rational mind. It works on the principle that a sudden impasse or jolt to the intellect can bring insight.

I believe that many Christian leaders are doing a Zen koan move on believers without realizing it. Their Scripture-twisting, double-talk, and taking verses out of context derails one's rational thinking. Sometimes after I read or listened to one of their teach-ings, I thought maybe it was Scriptural, until I looked up each verse. It was tedious to do, but when I examined each verse in context, I realized that the Scriptures had been twisted.

Develop Sensitivity and Awareness

Through martial arts training (before the Lord led me out), I had learned to develop my peripheral vision. When sparring I could focus on my opponent's eyes or chest area while simultaneously being able to see his hands and feet. This prepared me for what-ever attack he might use. I demonstrated this skill when I would go into schools to speak and do self-defense clinics. Looking at students in the center of the audience, I could tell them what other students were doing on both sides.

Many martial artists develop this type of sensitivity and awareness to the degree that they can sense or anticipate their opponent's attack as soon as it begins, and thereby effectively counter the attack. Some go even further. They try to become super sensitive through meditation and by developing the power of ki or ch'i. Their goal is to be able to think their opponent's thoughts and know his moves before he even begins the attack.

If a martial artist attempts to develop this much sensitivity to defeat an opponent, how much more should we develop a sensitivity and discernment by submission to the Lord, so He can guide and direct our lives through His Word and Spirit? The benefit of their mystical discernment is only temporary, while the implications of biblical discernment are eternal.

Seek to be an Expert on God's Word

The responsibility of every Christian is to seek to be an expert on the Word of God. Do not be too quick to accept every new teaching or technique, but examine all teachings, prophecies, revelations, and practices by the Word. When someone adds to, subtracts from, misinterprets, twists, or takes verses out of context in order to make them conform to their own ideas, you can examine the Scriptures in context and also apply other Scriptures to gain additional light on the subject. This will help you to accurately handle the Word of Truth (2 Timothy 2:15).

During my early ministry days, I found myself so absorbed in researching the cults, occult, and New Age that I spent more time reading books and magazines than I did God's Word, and it began to trouble me. So in 1989, after a time of intense prayer and fasting, and extensive Scripture study, I made a commitment to read His Word and pray three times a day. And except for valuable resource material, I gave most of my books away.

It has proven to be one of the most beneficial decisions I have ever made. Now instead of merely saying what this group, teacher, or "prophet" says, I know what God's Word says—and more importantly, I *know* the Author.

The pastor of an exciting and biblically balanced charismatic church in Minnesota, shared with me the following when I ministered there:

> One day in my quiet time the Lord challenged me to write down my six favorite verses, the ones I could quote by heart. I wrote down Mark 11:24; Philippians 4:13; 4:19; James 4:7; Hebrews 11:1; 1 Corinthians 1:27. After finishing I felt quite good about it. Then He challenged me to write down the subject and context of those verses. To my surprise I could not do it. When I looked them up I found that their meaning in context was entirely different than I had thought.
>
> Right then I determined to always know the context of a verse before I use it. That simple idea has revolutionized my thinking and ministry. You see, I thought the Church was in the midst of a "Word movement," and realized that it was only in the midst of a "verse movement."

A man writing to me from Australia concerning these "new" teachings and phenomena accurately stated: "When you take the *text* out of *context* you are left with *con*—and that is what is happening in our churches today."

Be a Berean (Acts 17:11) and evaluate everything said and done in light of God's Word, and if it is not accurate, reject it. Examine everything that comes into your mind whether it is from radio, television, the Internet, something you read, or from the pulpit. Make certain it is in accord with the Word of God. Let the Word—not your experience; let the Word—not evangelists, teachers, prophets, and apostles; let the Word—not someone's books and CDs—be your foundation.

The book of Revelation repeats five times that "the Word of God and the testimony of Jesus Christ" (Revelation 1:2; 1:9; 6:9; 12:17; 20:4) is of the utmost importance. Revelation 12:17 indicates that the dragon [Satan] was enraged—not at those who had subjective experiences but—at those "which keep the commandments of God, and have the testimony of Jesus Christ."

Joshua was commanded by God to: "Only be thou strong and very courageous, that thou mayest observe to do according to all the law, which Moses my servant commanded thee: turn not from it to the right hand or to the left, that thou mayest prosper withersoever thou goest. This book of the law shall not depart out of thy mouth; but thou shalt meditate therein day and night, that thou mayest observe to do according to all that is written therein: for then thou shalt make thy way prosperous, and then thou shalt have good success (Joshua 1:7, 8).

How much more should we totally build our lives on God's Word without turning to the right or to the left to follow extra-biblical and unbiblical revelations and experiences.

George O. Wood states:

I visited in Rome the prison from which Paul is believed to have written 2 Timothy prior to his own execution by Caesar. He would have been lowered into the cell through a hole in the ceiling. In the cold dampness of that dimly lit cell, his words brilliantly reach us today and illuminate our hearts. He closes the letter with a charge to Timothy and all Christian leaders: "PREACH THE WORD"

(2 Timothy 4:2)! He does not say, "Preach your own experience. Preach fads. Preach minor things as major things." No! He says: "PREACH THE WORD!" Why does he say that? Because "the time will come when men will not put up with sound doctrine" (2 Timothy 4:3).[25]

"King Saul Move"

I asked a pastor who had been attending various ministers' conferences where they are promoting some blatantly unscriptural teachings and practices, "Why are so many pastors getting involved?" He said, "The Church is hurting and this seems to be where all the excitement and growth is at." Such pastors are allowing popular New Age and occult techniques to infiltrate their churches and ministries, and they are seeing some excitement and growth.

They wrongly conclude: "It must be from God. There is so much love and unity. Things are going so well. The apparent blessings and prosperity confirm it is of God." But I say: "It is a deceptive 'satanic blessing' and is only temporary."

Many Christians are involved in what I call a "King Saul Move." King Saul started out obeying the Lord, and God greatly blessed him, until Saul began to disobey and rebel. When God no longer answered his prayers, King Saul went to the witch of Endor for advice. Instead he should have humbled himself, repented, and sought the Lord with all his heart.

Likewise, many Christians today are unwilling to repent and turn from hidden sins and false teachings and turn back to biblical Christianity with all their hearts. As a result they no longer hear God's voice and God no longer answers their prayers. They no longer walk in His presence, peace, and power. They become frustrated and discouraged. They think that the Bible is ineffective and the Lord has been unfaithful. They become vulnerable to false teachings and "new revelations" and phenomena that go contrary to the Scriptures. They allow popular New Age and occult techniques to infiltrate their churches and ministries.

But with each of these people, you can trace it back to decisions they made or involvements that were against God's will and in violation of biblical principles. Like Saul who went to the witch of Endor, many of these Christians involve themselves in New Age and occult techniques.

Why settle for an inferior, counterfeit technique when you can have the genuine power of God's Spirit? You can walk in God's presence and peace if you seek Him with all your heart. Before the Lord, I call you back to your First Love and to pure, unadulterated devotion to Him and His Word!

I don't care how many people tell you to believe something or how many Christian leaders are involved in this new technique or practice. It doesn't matter how many Christians are jumping on the bandwagon of this "new revelation." If it is not in accord with God's Word, reject it.

Over the years I have seen many "spiritual bandwagons" come and go. I have watched churches balloon with growth, excitement, and popularity for a season and then shrivel like a dried-out plant. Many are a shell of what they were before they welcomed in the false phenomena and practices. Their growth and glory was short lived.

I have watched too many pastors and Christians get "tossed to and fro, and carried about with every wind of doctrine, by the sleight of men, and cunning craftiness, whereby they lie in wait to deceive" (Ephesians 4:14). It is so much wiser to stay firmly grounded on the solid rock of God's Word.

Many Christians have had enough of all the new trends and gimmicks and desire the unadulterated preaching of God's Word. As a result, many churches proclaiming biblical Christianity are being filled with spiritually hungry and thirsty believers as they grow both numerically and in the *true* power and knowledge of the Lord Jesus Christ. God always preserves a faithful remnant.

Satan may be temporarily pouring out his spirit of deception and "blessing" among the apostate church, but God is pouring out among His faithful remnant a much greater anointing and resurrection power of His Spirit—the Spirit of Truth. Those who are His and who stay committed and true to His Word and Spirit will walk in greater power, authority, and victory than ever before.

Belshazzar's Final Fling

Belshazzar, king of Babylon, had a "final fling" in Daniel 5. So too, the apostate church is having her "final fling." While a lost and dying world goes to a Christ-less eternity, an excitement-crazed church "parties in the Spirit"—drunk, laughing, falling over, dancing sensually, involving themselves in New Age and occult techniques, and giving "new revelations" and "prophecies" that only encourage their foolish and errant ways. But the party is about to come to an end. The handwriting is on the wall.

Prophecy is being fulfilled. The New World Order and the deceptive temporary reign of Antichrist and the False Prophet loom on the horizon. Potential worldwide persecution and martyrdom of true believers in Christ draw ever closer. Apostasy accelerates, yet few seem to notice or care. The approaching tribulation of Antichrist's reign of terror, God's wrath and judgment, and Christ's second coming are ignored or distorted by supposed believers in Christ who are too busy partying and having a "good time in the Lord" to realize the signs of the times that are being fulfilled.

Concerning the end times Daniel 12:10 states: "Many shall be purified, and made white, and tried; but the wicked shall do wickedly: and none of the wicked shall understand; but the wise shall understand."

Belshazzar, who had been drinking wine, was unprepared for the attack of Darius the Mede and was slain by him. So too, a "church" drunk on the "new wine" will also be unprepared for what lies ahead, and will be "slain" with little resistance.

Belshazzar, who had become preoccupied with partying and feeling good, was oblivious to what was about to happen. But Daniel knew, and so will you know of the impending events that are to come in the last days, if you read the Word and get on your knees in prayer like he did. Doing so will help you have the same discernment and ultimate victory Daniel had.

David Wilkerson states it this way: "The Lord has a people in these confusing times who are not confused. They are so given to Jesus—so in love with Him, so open to the reproof of His Spirit, so separated from the wickedness of this age—that they know the ways and workings of the Holy Spirit. They know what is pure and holy, and what is fleshly and foolish..." [26]

In Daniel chapter 6, Daniel was appointed to leadership in Darius the Mede's new kingdom. Likewise, those who stay true to the Lord and honor His Word will be the ones whom God will eventually honor, vindicate, and empower.

When King Belshazzar offered Daniel great rewards for giving the interpretation of the handwriting on the wall, Daniel answered the king by saying: "Let thy gifts be to thyself, and give thy rewards to another; yet I will read the writing unto the king, and make known to him the interpretation" (Daniel 5:17).

I have had numerous opportunities throughout the years to compromise. I have been told that if I would just jump on the bandwagon of the current trends, I could have an even greater ministry and tremendous prosperity. My response is similar to Daniel's: Keep your gifts, keep your popularity. All I want is Jesus Christ. All I want is to walk in obedience to His Word. All I want is to walk in sensitivity and submission to the leading of His Spirit. I don't want anything the *world* has to offer in that regard. I've had my chance to have that, and I rejected it the way Moses rejected the riches of Egypt! When I gave my life to Christ, I gave up everything for Him. Why should I now—when we are so close to His return—sell Him out and go the convenient, popular way?

You can have your fleeting fame. You can have your temporary excitement and power. You can get involved in apostasy and enjoy the momentary pleasure of committing spiritual adultery. But there will be a time in the very near future when God's "handwriting" will be manifest and your face will grow pale and your knees will shake like Belshazzar's. Just as no conjurers or diviners could charm Belshazzar's dilemma away, no inner healing, visualization, positive confession, personal prophecy, "new revelation," imitation experience, or counterfeit miracle—not even a unified apostate church bent on world conquest—will be able to deliver you.

One day the popular, wealthy, and unified apostate church that makes those who dwell on earth drunk with the wine of her spiritual adultery will be destroyed. Revelation 17:16, 17 gives us the following account: "And the ten horns which thou sawest upon the beast, these shall hate the whore, and shall make her desolate and naked, and shall eat her flesh, and burn her with fire. For God hath put in their hearts to fulfil his will, and to agree, and give their kingdom unto the beast, until the words of God shall be fulfilled."

In contrast, true believers in Christ—those committed to the testimony of Jesus and obedient to the Word of God—will rule and reign with Christ for all eternity.

A small faithful church may seem less successful in man's eyes than a large compromised one. However, from God's perspective, success is not based on numbers but on faithfulness.

More Blatant Forms of Occultism

A man came into our ministry center requesting information on Halloween. From the conversation I discovered he was in leadership in a church propagating many of the techniques and beliefs I am exposing in this book. I asked, "How can you discern the spirit of occultism in Halloween, but you cannot discern the spirit of occultism that has infiltrated your church?" He had no real answer.

Christians who have become lukewarm and don't know God's Word, lack discernment and are getting involved in New Age and occult beliefs and techniques. They will eventually, if they do not repent, get into more blatant forms of occultism. Unless they repent, this very mentality and spirit could one day result in their taking the mark of the beast. This is a strong statement, but this gradual but continual undermining of many people's commitment to the Christ of the Bible is resulting in a growing tolerance and acceptance of New Age and occult beliefs and practices.

Many years ago I said that we would one day see churches that once loved the Lord committing spiritual adultery by bringing occultism into the church. We are now seeing it. Many have replaced commitment to the Christ of the Bible and obedience to God's Word and the genuine moving of God's Spirit with occult, New Age techniques and beliefs that they have tried to Christianize and justify.

Initially, what many thought were new insights from God's Word are now becoming more and more occult in nature, exposing their true source and inspiration.

We will soon see blatant occultism, sexual immorality, lewd dancing, and other fleshly and demonic manifestations around the altars of many churches. Many church services will more resemble the revelry around the golden calf in Exodus 32 than a gathering of New Testament Spirit-filled believers. The words written about Aaron in Exodus 32:25 will be true of many pastors: "Now when Moses saw that the people were unrestrained (for Aaron had not restrained them, to their shame among their enemies)" (NKJV).

Believers who are participating in New Age and occult beliefs and practices must repent and turn away from them. Return to sound Scriptural beliefs and practices—or drift further and further from the truth.

We're Called to Purity—Not Adultery

Many are rising up in Christ's name and seducing His bride into spiritual adultery through false prophecies, pseudo-miracles, and occult phenomena. Deception and error is rampant in the body of Christ.

I feel like Paul, who said in 2 Corinthians 11:2–4: "For I am jealous over you with godly jealousy: for I have espoused you to one husband, that I may present you as a chaste virgin to Christ. But I fear, lest by any means, as the serpent beguiled Eve through his subtilty, so your minds should be corrupted from the simplicity that is in Christ. For if he that cometh preacheth another Jesus, whom we have not preached, or if ye receive another spirit, which ye have not received, or another gospel, which ye have not accepted, ye might well bear with him.

What is one reason in the New Testament why you can divorce your wife? Adultery. Do you know why in the Old Testament that God temporarily separated Himself from Israel? It was because of spiritual adultery—unfaithfulness to Him and His Word.

When the Israelites were obedient and followed the Lord with all their hearts, they had blessings and security. But when they were disobedient and followed other gods, they had famines, lost wars, and eventually went into captivity.

He let Israel (the ten northern tribes) go into Assyrian captivity (722 B.C.), and He let Judah be taken into Babylonian captivity (586 B.C.) for one main reason—spiritual adultery.

God created us to have a relationship with Him, to be His bride. When God sees His bride being a prostitute by committing spiritual adultery, it offends and angers Him in the same way it would hurt and anger you if your mate was unfaithful to you.

Hosea says concerning God's people: "...for the spirit of whoredoms hath caused them to err, and they have gone a whoring from under their God" (Hosea 4:12).

In fact the entire book of Hosea deals with Israel's harlotry,

NOT OUR FATHER'S FAITH

God's judgment because of it, and God's forgiveness and restoration. A few other Scriptures which reveal God's displeasure with spiritual adultery are: Leviticus 20:6; Psalm 106:35–40; Jeremiah 3:1–25; Ezekiel 16:1–43; 23:1–49; Revelation 17:1–19:2.

Be Hot or Cold, but Not Lukewarm

In Revelation 3:15–19, the resurrected Christ gives a relevant message for the body of Christ today. He says:

> I know thy works, that thou art neither cold nor hot: I would thou wert cold or hot. So then because thou art lukewarm, and neither cold nor hot, I will spue thee out of my mouth. Because thou sayest, I am rich, and increased with goods, and have need of nothing; and knowest not that thou art wretched, and miserable, and poor, and blind, and naked: I counsel thee to buy of me gold tried in the fire, that thou mayest be rich; and white raiment, that thou mayest be clothed, and that the shame of thy nakedness do not appear; and anoint thine eyes with eyesalve, that thou mayest see. As many as I love, I rebuke and chasten: be zealous therefore, and repent.

God is saying to you today that if you want to compromise and be lukewarm, then you can have your temporary pleasure. But He would rather you serve Him with all your heart. Do not be lukewarm. Do not have that unholy mix ("the cup of the Lord and the cup of demons," 1 Corinthians 10:21) by using His name and twisting His Word and then seducing His people into occultism, New Ageism, and spiritual adultery. Come out from among those who are lukewarm and spiritual prostitutes.

Three Woes

It is in searching the Scripture, fasting, and prayer that I hear from the Lord. During such a time the Lord spoke to my heart that one of my main desires and prayers should be: "Lord, use me to turn the hearts of Your people back to You, or let me die trying." I had it put on a poster and hung it in my office as a continual reminder.

In Matthew 23, Jesus gave several woes. And in keeping with that theme, I want to list for you three warnings to the body of Christ that the Lord strongly impressed upon my heart and mind on an occasion of being on my knees before Him in prayer and fasting:

1) Woe to you who replace walking in obedience to God's Word and receiving the genuine transforming power of His Holy Spirit, with psychospiritual techniques, emotionalism, mind control, occult techniques, or pseudo-miracles!

2) Woe to you who attempt to manipulate God or usurp His Lordship by confessing your own will instead of seeking and submitting to His!

3) Woe to you who prophesy falsely and of your own inspiration, or who seek and follow the word of a "prophet" and "new revelations" more than you seek and follow the Word of God!

Repent and return to the Lord with your whole heart. Return to obedience to His Word and Spirit.

Keep On Course with Discernment

I was speaking at a convention in the Himalayas during my first India outreach. We had to walk on mountain trails from where we were staying at the orphanage to get to the convention site. At night it was so dark we had to use flashlights.

The last night of the convention I decided to stay back at the orphanage by myself to spend some extra time in prayer before my final message. When it was time for me to go, I realized it was almost pitch black, with just a little light from the moon and stars. So I walked the mountain trail alone with just a small flashlight. It is amazing how a trail that takes five minutes to walk in the daytime becomes so difficult to walk at night, especially when you are all by yourself.

By then the convention was already going on. They were singing and I was supposed to be the featured speaker, so I prayed, "Lord, it is going to be a little bit of an adventure. You have to help me take the correct path and get there on time."

I had to do two things to keep myself on course. First, I had to be very sensitive to my environment. I had to shine my flashlight onto my path and watch for trees, rocks, a narrow wooden bridge over a mountain stream, and other sign posts I could recognize, to make certain I was going the right way. I also had to feel with my feet so I did not fall over any of the many rocks scattered along the way.

Secondly, I had to be very sensitive to listen to the singing to make certain the path I was taking was getting me closer and closer to the convention site. I also had to be sensitive to hear the sound of running water, so I would know I was going over the right mountain stream, confirmed by the other signposts.

Many trails in the mountains intersect each other. It was imperative that I take the correct trail, not only so I could make it to the convention, but also because one wrong turn could cause me to be lost in the Himalayas all night, and possibly freeze to death.

So too, today, there are many "intersecting" spiritual teachings, techniques, and experiences. We, therefore, must know the "environment" of God's Word and must have a sensitivity to and discernment from God's Spirit.

I had to recognize the trees and bridges, and feel around the paths with my feet for rocks, and shine my flashlight on the trail to get to the right location (because to go in the wrong direction could be disastrous). We must know God's Word which "is a lamp to my feet, and a light to my path" (Psalm 119:105), so that we will follow the right path lest we end up in spiritual chaos.

In the same way I had to listen for the running water and listen for the singing, we have to be tuned-in and sensitive to God's Spirit—not to our own inspiration, not to things we want to interpret as being God's Spirit, and not to a counterfeit voice. That only comes by getting into His Word, getting on our knees in prayer and fasting, and by seeking His will with all our hearts. That is what God is calling the body of Christ to do today!

Joshua's Challenge to Only Serve the Lord

After Joshua reviewed many of the great things the Lord had done for the people (Joshua 24:1–13), he challenged them to: "fear the

LORD, and serve him in sincerity and in truth: and put away the gods which your fathers served on the other side of the flood, and in Egypt; and serve ye the LORD. And if it seem evil unto you to serve the LORD, choose you this day whom ye will serve; whether the gods which your fathers served that were on the other side of the flood, or the gods of the Amorites, in whose land ye dwell: but as for me and my house, we will serve the LORD" (Joshua 24:14, 15).

It was a time for Joshua and the people of Israel to reflect on where they had been, and how God had delivered and preserved them through the trials of the wilderness and the lands of hostile foreign peoples. They recalled how the Lord drove out all their enemies from the land before them. Joshua reminded the Hebrews, however, of God's holiness; that He is a jealous God who will not put up with spiritual adultery.

He declared: "If ye forsake the LORD, and serve strange gods, then he will turn and do you hurt, and consume you, after that he hath done you good" (Joshua 24:20).

The people committed to Joshua that they would serve the Lord (Joshua 24:21). Joshua then challenged them to therefore "put away, said he, the strange gods which are among you, and incline your heart unto the LORD God of Israel" (Joshua 24:23). That very day Joshua made a covenant with the people concerning their commitment to only serve the Lord (Joshua 24:24–27). Further instruction on this matter comes to us from the book of Samuel: "And Samuel spake unto all the house of Israel, saying, If ye do return unto the LORD with all your hearts, then put away the strange gods and Ashtaroth from among you, and prepare your hearts unto the LORD, and serve him only: and he will deliver you out of the hand of the Philistines" (1 Samuel 7:3).

Take the TV Challenge!

I have challenged many pastors and believers to turn off their televisions for one month. I tell them, "Don't watch any TV or movies, or listen to Christian CDs, or read Christian books, or attend any Christian seminars or conferences. And stay off the Internet. Instead of getting filtered Scriptural teaching, for just one month read only the Word of God and spend time in prayer and fasting."

Those who have taken the challenge have frequently informed me that this process has helped them see that many of the current teachings, techniques, and phenomena are not Scriptural, and as a result they make a renewed commitment to biblical Christianity.

When I started into the ministry, I learned that I was not to emulate the great evangelists, or popular preachers, or even my favorite missionaries. Instead of trying to become like them, God showed me that I was to build my life and ministry on the Bible and the leading of His Spirit.

So I turned to the Scriptures, and as I did, I prayed: "Lord, show me what characteristics and qualities You require of those who are to serve You. What do YOU want?" He showed me in the lives of the heroes of the faith and also through those who failed. It was by examining their lives that I learned those things that are pleasing to God and those things He finds repulsive.

Throughout my ministry I have prayed, "Lord, don't let me attempt to manipulate You into what I want or think You should be, but reveal Yourself to me as You are. I want to know You. Make known to me who You are by Your Word and by Your Spirit, then cause me to submit and be conformed to who You are and what You require of me." I also ask the Lord to "Enable me to stand for the things You stand for and oppose the things You oppose. Teach me to love the things You love and hate the things You hate."

The Lord has transformed me from a rebellious teenager to a man who desires more than anything else in this world to know and please Him. The only explanation for this transformation is that God changed me through the principles in His Word and the power of His Holy Spirit. Had I not spent time in prayer and fasting and studying His Word, my life would have remained unchanged.

Do you want to be a biblical Christian and know if today's trends and phenomena are of God or not? Then I challenge you to turn off the TV for one month. Listen to, and read only the Bible in your pursuit of knowing God and His Truth.

You will have a new perspective on life and current trends. You will discern what is from God and what is not. You will be on your way to building your life and ministry on biblical Christianity. The rewards will be far greater than you can imagine, and far superior to any new revelation, teaching, technique, or phenomena. You will walk in greater peace, power, and victory than you ever dreamed possible.

Biblical Christianity begins with:

- knowing the Word (Christ is the Word, John 1);
- knowing the God who inspired that Word;
- and by being empowered by His Holy Spirit.

When these three aspects of the Christian life are operative in you, you will discern deception and be a bold witness for Him and His Truth.

When You Know the Genuine—
You'll Spot the Counterfeit

By the time you finish reading this book, there will probably be more false teachings, fads, and phenomena entering the church—most likely "old" forms in "new" garb.

So beware of the subtle errors that so easily capture the hearts and minds of the unsuspecting. Get to know the genuine by studying the Word of God and you will be able to identify the imitation and the counterfeit and lead others to a knowledge of the Truth.

Know the authentic Holy Spirit revealed in Scripture and you will have spiritual discernment to guard your mind and your heart against the corrupt teachings of those who are "deceiving and being deceived" (2 Timothy 3:13).

As a watchman, I have sounded the alarm and have warned the body of Christ. I have obeyed what Scripture instructs and what the Holy Spirit has led me to do. The choice is now yours. It is between you and the Lord.

My closing words to you are those of Paul to the Corinthians: "Watch, stand fast in the faith, be brave, be strong. Let all that you do be done with love" (1 Corinthians 16:13, 14 NKJV).

Other Books by Bill Rudge:

OVERCOMING SEXUAL IMMORALITY

Struggling with sexual issues? Then read this hard hitting and practical book. Drawing upon years of research and ministry experience, Bill Rudge exposes the problem of living an undisciplined sex-life and offers scriptural solutions that will help you overcome sexual immorality.

Chapters include:
- The Sexual Fantasy World Is Far from Reality
- But We're in Love
- The Bondage of Pornography
- The Media Connection
- Even Heroes Suffer Consequences
- God's Perspective
- Steps to Overcoming Sexual Immorality
- A Storybook Romance
- A Modern Day Love Story

WHO IS THIS JESUS

This easy-to-read, yet profound book by Bill Rudge will equip you to answer tough questions. It is an excellent witnessing tool for sharing Jesus Christ with Jews, Muslims, Hindus, New Agers, and anyone searching for truth. Discover many convincing proofs and find answers to such challenging questions as:

- Is there more than one Christ?
- How can we know who the true Messiah is?

- Are there many ways to God?
- Is Jesus God?
- Was the crucifixion a mistake?
- Is there evidence for the resurrection?
- Will Jesus return?
- How can you *know* Him?

THE LAST DAYS

We are living at the most exciting time in the history of the world. Our generation has the potential more than any other generation to see the fulfillment of Revelation. Bill Rudge reveals what's ahead for the body of Christ, the apostate church, and the world as he demonstrates from God's Word the irrefutable signs that Christ's return is near.

Some topics are:
- Seven Mountain Peaks of Bible Prophecy
- Signs of the Times
- Mark of the Beast
- Global Society
- Unity of Religion
- Increasing Persecution
- Apostate Church
- Defeat of Antichrist
- God Has it All Under Control

**This book is an eye-opener.
It will stir you to readiness.**

FASTING FOR SENSITIVITY AND POWER

Bill Rudge has challenged thousands of believers and Christian leaders to fast. This popular booklet will equip you to master the ancient biblical principles of fasting, which have so greatly impacted Bill's life and ministry.

It will teach you:
- Why to fast
- How to fast
- How to prepare to fast
- How to pray during a fast
- How to end a fast

SPIRITUAL WARFARE AND VICTORY IN CHRIST

As soon as you give your life to Jesus Christ, you enter the arena of spiritual warfare. Your former peaceful coexistence with the forces of darkness terminates. Read *Spiritual Warfare and Victory in Christ* by Bill Rudge to discover how to become effective in spiritual warfare.

Topics include:
- The Arena
- Know Your Enemy
- Scripture Condemns Sorcery
- The Need for Balance
- Pattern of Spiritual Warfare in Scripture
- The Armor of God

- Spiritual Warfare Likened to Physical Combat
- Delegated Authority
- Christ's Power Versus Satan's
- Conversion of a Voodoo Witch Doctor
- Victory in Christ

REACHING YOUR MAXIMUM POTENTIAL IN CHRIST

This powerful and popular book by Bill Rudge has impacted the lives of countless youth and adults—military personnel, prisoners, athletes, and people in almost every facet of life. It contains timeless scriptural principles and is laced with exciting illustrations of how they have been put to the test in real life experiences.

Chapters include:
- Examine the Evidence
- Count the Cost
- Total Commitment
- Obedience
- Surrendered
- Motives
- Integrity
- Balanced Life
- Self-Control—the Essence of Strength
- Courage to Stand Alone
- Determination to Never Give Up
- Hidden Sins
- Desire the Lord
- Take the Challenge

NOTES

1. Interview by Russell Chandler, *Paul McGuire: Escaping the New Age, Charisma & Christian Life,* Strang Communications Co., May 1989, p. 65.

2. Johanna Michaelsen, *Like Lambs to the Slaughter,* Harvest House Publishers, Eugene, OR, 1989, p. 123.

3. Napoleon Hill, *Think and Grow Rich,* Random House, pp. 213, 214, 215, 217, 218.

4. Martin L. Rossman, M.D., *The Healing Power of Imagery, New Age Journal,* March/April 1988, pp. 53-56.

5. Kurt Koch, *Occult ABC,* Kregel Publications, Grand Rapids, MI, 1978, p. 95.

6. Wilson & Weldon, *Occult Shock,* Master Books, San Diego, CA, 1980, pp. 227, 228.

7. Peter & Patti Lalonde, eds., *Omega Letter,* Ontario, Canada, vol. 2:10, Nov. 1987.

8. Lawrence O. Richards, *Expository Dictionary of Bible Words,* Zondervan Publishing House, Grand Rapids, MI, 1985, pp. 505, 507.

9. Donald Gee, *Concerning Spiritual Gifts,* Gospel Publishing House, Springfield, MO, pp. 43, 44.

10. *People & Events, Charisma & Christian Life,* Feb. 1990, p. 16.

11. Donald C. Stamps, ed., *The Full Life Study Bible,* Zondervan Publishing House, Grand Rapids, MI, "Introduction: Jeremiah," 1992, p. 1079.

12. Bill Rudge, *A Cult & 'Extreme Group' Awareness Alphabet,* Bill Rudge Ministries, Hermitage, PA, 1982, pp. 24, 25.

13. *The Full Life Study Bible,* from I Corinthians14:24 footnote, p. 1775.

14. W. Phillip Keller, *Predators In Our Pulpits,* Harvest House Publishers, Eugene, OR, 1988, pp. 77, 78.

15. David Wilkerson, *Times Square Church Pulpit Series,* Sept. 1995.

16. David A. Sabella— Taken from preliminary Greek exegesis research developed for the paper: *An Exegetical Study of Ephesians 5:19 and Colossians 3:16,* for M.Div. requirement at Reformed Presbyterian Theological Seminary, May, 1995.

17. George A. Buttrick, ed., *The Interpreter's Bible,* Volume X, Abingdon Press, Nashville, TN, 1953, p. 714.

18. Excerpted from: *Rabindranath R. Maharaj (with Dave Hunt), Death of A Guru,* A. J. Holman Company, Philadelphia, PA, 1977. Tal Brooke (research by John Weldon), *Riders of the Cosmic Circuit,* Lion Publishing, England, 1986.

19. *Spiritual Counterfeits Project Newsletter,* Volume 19:4, SCP, Inc., Spring 1995, p. 8.

20. *Spiritual Counterfeits Project Newsletter,* Volume 19:2, Fall 1994, p. 14.

21. Ibid.

22. Ibid.

23. Ibid.

24. Johanna Michaelsen, *The Beautiful Side of Evil,* Harvest House Publishers, Eugene, OR, 1982, pp. 179, 183, 184.

25. George O. Wood, Unpublished Article: *The Laughing Revival,* Springfield, MO, 1995.

26. David Wilkerson, *Times Square Church Pulpit Series,* Sept. 1995.

FOR MORE INFORMATION:

Bill Rudge has produced numerous books, pamphlets, and CDs on a variety of timely topics. For a complete listing or a copy of his informative newsletter, visit our web site: www.billrudge.org

or write to:

Bill Rudge Ministries

P.O. Box 108

Sharon, PA 16146 U.S.A.